The Business of Research
Issues of Policy and Practice

T0324248

The Business of Research
Issues of Policy and Practice

Catherine Jones Finer and Gillian Lewando Hundt

Copyright © Blackwell Publishers Ltd 2001

This edition first published 2001

Blackwell Publishers Ltd
108 Cowley Road
Oxford OX4 1JF, UK

Blackwell Publishers Inc
350 Main Street
Malden, Massachusetts 02148, USA

British Library Cataloguing in Publication Data has been applied for

Library of Congress Cataloging in Publication Data has been applied for

ISBN 0–631–22824–1 (pbk)

Typeset by Graphicraft Ltd, Hong Kong
Printed and bound in Great Britain
by MPG Books Ltd, Bodmin, Cornwall

This book is printed on acid-free paper

CONTENTS

INTRODUCTION

Catherine Jones Finer and Gillian Lewando Hundt

We chose the title for this collection with care. Modern research practice is a far cry from the ideal type of the dedicated scholar-scientist selflessly pursuing an independent line of enquiry in an unceasing quest for knowledge and understanding. It is a business activity: not merely in the sense that it is about securing financial backing and thence delivering to order, but in the sense that the entire intervening research operation has also, somehow, to be "managed". Without question there are different styles and examples of management to be drawn on and learnt from, just as in any other field of business enterprise. But this is not something the academic community so far appears to have come to terms with, to any convincing extent.

Academics are trained to write about research findings and research methods. Whereas reflecting on the actual process and conduct of research is *not* commonly something they have been trained to do. Indeed, writing reflexively about oneself and one's colleagues—not to mention one's funding agencies—can be a risky business. It is not easy to find the appropriate language, framework or tone. There is no wish to place future funding at risk or to offend colleagues. Furthermore, there has typically been no time or money set aside to cover for such longer-term, beyond-the-immediate-project, forms of activity. The award of a Leverhulme Fellowship to one of the editors, precisely to enable her to reflect on a recent major research experience, stands in glaring exception to the general rule.

Nevertheless it is the *management* of research which is taking up more and more of the time of senior academics who, in consequence, are tending less and less to be involved in actual data collection in the field. Rather they are spending time learning about funders' priorities; writing proposals; liaising with co-researchers; recruiting, training and managing staff; and writing up and disseminating findings. All such activities are normally absent from formal debate and publications, and require skills which are not taught as part of formal postgraduate training. It is the purpose of this volume to begin to make good this deficiency, at least in respect of Social Policy—as ever, broadly interpreted.

The contributors are all conscious of this gap in the research literature and have each struggled to find a way in which to put across their experience to best effect. All of them are "British-based", as are most of the funding agencies—aside from the European Commission—to which they refer. The list is (for Britain) comprehensive: including such public bodies as the Department for International Development, the Economic and Social Research Council, the Scottish Office, the Home Office and the Association of Probation Committees, together with such key charities as the Leverhulme and Joseph Rowntree Trusts and the Nuffield Foundation. Nevertheless, this is not in any other sense to be described as a "British collection". The reach and scale of the projects referred to varies from the most localized to the most internationally far-flung. The fields covered range from health care to homelessness, from probation to conservation, from social care to social history. Most importantly, the issues raised are generic rather than project-specific. Irrespective of the dimensions of a particular project, the reader will find common themes recurring, both practical and ethical. For instance, the significance of interpersonal and interprofessional relations—as between consultants and researchers, different teams of researchers, or between researcher and researched—stands out as a recurrent theme. Then again, some of the authors are using as "data" correspondence between themselves and colleagues and/or volunteer supporters, which raises issues of consent. Whereas respondents sign consent forms, colleagues and volunteer supporters do not. Yet consent for the use of correspondence is, in principle, essential. With regard to most of this collection, such permissions have been requested in the course of the preparation of each paper whereas, in the case of Finer's researches into a contemporary archive, this was simply not practicable; the only possibility in this case being either to so disguise the origins of any correspondence as to render its author unidentifiable—or else to leave any "too attributable" correspondence altogether out of the count. Such are some of the awkwardnesses of the business of research, itself and themselves fast acquiring global significance.

Taking Britain as a "case example": our failure to recruit a senior academic of relevant experience to comment freely on the conduct of the periodic Research Assessment Exercise (RAE) to which university departments and their "research-relevant" staff are now subject, was significant though hardly surprising. The academics approached invariably turned out to be either involved in the conduct of the current RAE exercise in which case their lips were sealed; or else—"please understand"—to be mindful of ongoing prospects for research funding, on the part of themselves, their colleagues and/or their universities, such as might be jeopardized by any ill-judged, "ill-timed" outpouring of *realspeak* on their part; or else, finally, to be so jaded by their experiences of the recent past as to wish to put it all behind them.

It is in the light of such realities that we are especially appreciative of Janet Lewis's opening contribution. As Director of Research for the Joseph Rowntree Foundation ("the largest independent funder of social science research whose resources do not derive from public funds"; Joseph Rowntree Foundation 1999: 1), she offers a rare, informed, wide-ranging and above all *independent* review of the state of research funding as seen "from the top". The mismatch between traditional concepts of the scholar academic—expected always to be able to fuel teaching with the products of personal research—versus the commonplace of today's mostly team- and contract-based, commissioned research, is nicely portrayed, as is the mismatch between the RAE's declared commitment to "user-oriented useful research" and its distinctly *non*-user-oriented ranking of individual (rather than group) research outputs, based on traditional notions of "academic merit".

The following cluster of papers is "international" in the obvious sense that the scope of the fieldwork—and thence of the parties involved in the research—has, by definition, been just that. They are here ranked "in order of process", in the sense that they tend to highlight particular issues associated with particular stages in this level of research. Thus Ogden and Porter expose the structure of collaborative international health research as funded by the Overseas Development Administration/Department for International Development in the field of tuberculosis, and raise issues concerning the development of *partnerships* between, in this case, UK "consultants" and Indian researchers. Ettorre then turns our attention to the role of the *coordinator* in an international health research project involving partners from a range of countries—a structure which is common to EC-funded research. She discusses the difficulties of language, the contrasting understandings of the role of a coordinator, and the ways in which she resolved some of these issues during the course of the research. Next, Chatty explores the role and scope for an outside consultant to introduce indigenous *participation* into, in this case, a development project in conservation. Government planning of a nature conservation project had ignored the views of indigenous Bedouin in Syria. She identifies general issues in the conflict between conservation and indigenous rights, delineates the local policy background, then describes her own careful attempts to nurture a dialogue between civil servants and Bedouin pastoralists. Finally, Lewando Hundt concentrates on problems of disseminating research findings simultaneously in local, national and international terms, in respect of an EC-funded international research project in health and health care, whose various players/stakeholders had already evinced multiple, different understandings of the research project's findings and their possible significance. She delineates the discourses being contested and sets out the ways in which some of the key differences were subjected to negotiation.

After this, Finer's sustained encounter with a contemporary archive offers, in effect, a bridge from the "international" to the "local" in this collection. Her research concerned the records of a charismatically-led "good cause" based in Naples; yet her own interest centred on this same organization's international network of fundraisers (British in particular), as sustained over nearly half a century. The local and the international were thus in constant, often tortuous, juxtaposition. Third's account of researching homelessness in Scotland then follows on from this to the extent not merely of its being another study to do with the "dispossessed", but because of the fresh range of issues, both practical and ethical, raised by what was *par excellence* an empirical fieldwork rather than an archival undertaking.

The final three papers tackle the vexed question of how—and on what terms—researchers might "simultaneously" be expected to help bring about changes in policy and operational practice. Each is understandably conscious of the risks involved, both for themselves and for those with whom they have to liaise. Yet all declare themselves convinced that the exercise *can* work, provided the start-up arrangements are right and there is scope for ongoing mutual adjustment in the light of experience. Kemshall adopts a robust approach by designating "action research" as just one possible approach to ethical and political dilemmas in "offender risk research", for all that it cannot of itself resolve problems of "differential power and social relations between researcher and researched". Bate, by contrast, concentrates much more thoroughly upon the evolving dynamics of action research *per se*, as viewed, in his case, from the perspective of an anthropologist commissioned to participate in reforming the interpersonal workings of a hospital. Waterson, finally, and by contrast again, writes from recent personal experience on the questionable role of the action researcher *per se*: in her case being someone who inherited the research undertaking with the job; whose limited understanding of what is involved and/or what might be achieved is not so much shared as *matched* by the no less limited understanding of the social services "colleagues" with whom she was contracted to liaise.

In short, this is a worthwhile, stimulating collection.

Catherine Jones Finer
Gillian Lewando Hundt

Postscript
Since its original publication of this editorial in December 2000, the journal *Social Policy & Administration* has been informed by the Press and Parliamentary Officer of the **Social Policy Association**, Professor Gary Craig, that 'The Social Policy Association, which represents the interests of the academic and related communities, funded, supported and published enquiries into the conduct of the 1992 and 1996 RAEs, the former written by Dr Angus Erskine now of the University of Stirling and Professor Clare Ungerson now of the University of Southampton (and who is now a member of the 2001 Panel), the latter by myself. The findings of these studies, which were appropriately critical, were widely disseminated, not least at a national workshop convened in 1998. The **SPA** continues to engage in a robust debate with the RAE social policy panel and has had some lively discussions at national conferences and in meetings with members of the panel. These discussions are open to all. . . .'

Gary Craig,
Professor of Social Justice,
University of Hull, HU6 7RX.

The full text of Professor Craig's message may be obtained from Blackwell Publishers. Please contact the Journal Managing Editor for Social Policy and Administration.

I

Funding Social Science Research in Academia

Janet Lewis

Keywords

Research; Funding; Assessment; User involvement

Introduction

Doing research is a growing activity. The growth of the knowledge economy encourages everyone to want to know more and to find out more. As manual tasks are automated and carried out by machines, so more people move into the tertiary and quaternary sectors of the labour market, to work in the service and knowledge industries. But many of the structures through which we fund research are not necessarily geared up to this expansion. There remains an underlying assumption that research is carried out by individual scholars, if not in a garret or at the feet of great thinkers, then as part of individual academic endeavour. This is no longer appropriate as the norm.

There are considerable variations between disciplines in the way in which research is organized and managed. This paper will focus particularly on the social sciences. The sums of money spent on social science research are considerably less than the funds available for the physical and medical sciences. This is probably because social science is a much younger discipline. In some quarters there is a view that because social science is not laboratory-based it can be carried out more cheaply than the traditional sciences. The social sciences do use a variety of methods and it is possible to carry out qualitative work on a relatively small scale. But some social science research requires substantial sums of money, for example for longitudinal surveys, or studies which are attempting to evaluate the outcomes of particular interventions. Social science research is underfunded, but within the scientific and funding establishment social science demands tend to be seen as not as important as those of "big science".

The Different Streams of Research Funding

There are a variety of ways in which research is funded within the academic sphere.

Janet Lewis

1. Pre-eminent for academics is funding from the Higher Education Fund-
    ing Councils. In earlier decades such money was allocated on a block-
    grant basis but since the late 1980s, with the introduction of Research
    Assessment Exercises, funding has been selective and linked to perform-
    ance. The year 2001 will see the fifth such exercise, earlier ones having
    been carried out in 1986, 1989, 1992 and 1996.
2. Research councils: the SSRC and then ESRC have shifted over the
    years from operating a grant-giving, predominantly responsive-mode ap-
    proach, to a much more directed stance. This has partly been a response
    to pressure from government to be much more concerned about the
    usefulness of research. There has also been a shift away from individual
    project funding towards programmes of work and support for Centres
    within universities focused on particular topics or areas of work. There
    remains the possibility of funding individual pieces of work, through the
    Grants Board. In 2000 the ESRC's budget for research is £42 million of
    which £15 million is available for the responsive research grant scheme.
3. Charitable foundations: the social science foundations are relatively
    small players compared with those in the medical field. For example, the
    budget of the Wellcome Trust in 1996/7 was £227 million. The Joseph
    Rowntree Foundation, which is the charitable trust with the largest budget
    for social science research, is committing around £9 million in 2000,
    while the Nuffield Foundation which is the other main funder for research
    spent £6.4 million in 1997. The Leverhulme Trust had a bigger overall
    budget of £15.24 million in 1997 but only spends a proportion of its
    funds on social science with the bulk going to the humanities and
    medicine. There are some newish players in this field such as the
    National Lottery Charities Board (NLCB) which has had two rounds of
    funding research on health and disability. Out of a total budget of around
    £285 million in 1999, the NLCB spent around £20 million on health
    and social research. The medical insurance group PPP has also just set
    up a charitable foundation. Disposable income in 1999 was around
    £17 million which funded medical research and the education and train-
    ing of people providing health care; some social science research con-
    cerned with "the relief of sickness and disability and the relief of the
    aged"; and public health initiatives.
        In general the charitable foundations support research as part of a
    mission to change the world, rather than to pursue knowledge for its
    own sake (apart from the Leverhulme Trust whose aim is to do just
    that). While these foundations are concerned to ensure that the work
    will be carried out to a rigorous standard and will be acceptable scientific-
    ally, the topic is also of relevance to whether the project is supported.
    The JRF has moved in a similar direction to the research councils in
    that the majority of the projects it supports are part of programmes of
    work that have agreed priorities, rather than being unsolicited proposals
    within broad topic areas. The Nuffield Foundation has moved in this
    direction as far as a proportion of its work is concerned.
4. Work commissioned by government departments, NHS research and
    development, local government and the private sector: governments

vary as to the extent to which they wish policy to be based on up-to-date knowledge. The current government is giving great emphasis to "evidence-based practice"—at least as far as their public statements are concerned and the research budgets of many central government departments have been increased in the last few years. Devolution has also seen an increased emphasis on research focused on and in Scotland, and to a certain extent Wales. The NHS Executive has developed its research role in recent times while quangos and local authorities also fund a range of research projects. The private sector does not seem to be a major funder of research within the majority of the social sciences—economics and business studies are probably exceptions. This is probably because key social policy issues are seen to be the responsibility of the public sector.

Who Research Is For

Where a piece of research is commissioned by an external body, it is pretty clear who it is being carried out for. Private and public sector bodies are probably funding research in order to find out something or increase their knowledge of an issue of direct relevance to them. Most charitable foundations are funding research as a means to an end and are seeking knowledge either for themselves or for the wider audiences they hope to benefit. What has been changing over the years is the view of the purpose of research carried out with Higher Education and Research Council funding. The previous Conservative government, through its White Paper *Realizing our potential* (Chancellor of the Duchy of Lancaster 1993), set out its expectations that research councils should give more attention to the views and perspectives of "users" and "beneficiaries" and put stress on the utility of research. The Higher Education Funding Councils are now assuming that "relevance" is important to their mission. For example an April 2000 consultation document from the Scottish Higher Education Funding Council concerned with "Research and the knowledge age" identified as one of its objectives "the development of new research capacity and strengths, particularly where this has the potential to meet the long-term needs of Scotland" (Scottish Higher Education Funding Council 2000).

David Blunkett in the ESRC Lecture Speech of 2 February 2000 called on the academic community to do better and more relevant research. He talked of the frustration caused by a tendency for research: to address issues other than those which are central and directly relevant to the political and policy debate; to fail to take account of the reality of many people's lives; and sometimes to be driven by ideology paraded as intellectual inquiry or critique (Blunkett 2000). These views suggest a minister firmly in the "research to provide information" camp, rather than "research as a contribution to increasing knowledge and understanding". As such, it is a straightforward and perhaps simplistic view of the relationship between research and policy making.

While "relevance" is being given greater emphasis there continue to be pressures to assess research proposals on traditional criteria. For example, the recently appointed chief executive of the ESRC, Gordon Marshall, is quoted as having said that he expects the ESRC to maintain high standards of scientific excellence when deciding what proposals to fund. Combining relevance and science are not incompatible but this trend towards "utility" raises some important questions.

1. Are we losing the capacity to fund research which has no obvious current utility? I think that the sociology and history of science is full of examples of major intellectual breakthroughs that came about through research—and other activities—which started with no expectation that they would address the issue that emerged.
2. What is the consequence of the shift from the "bottom-up" generation of ideas for research, which is the essence of the *responsive mode* of research funding, to the "top-down" identification of topics which is increasingly prevalent? Will the health of the social science community be reduced in the long term if an increasing proportion of research funds are for pieces of work specified by people who are not researchers—or not social scientists? Creating a class of professional "jobbing" researchers may improve the delivery of completed commissioned projects, but reduce inspiration, innovation and new thinking, whether for theoretical or "relevant" work. We need to maintain a capacity to support intellectual curiosity and to be funding some people to pursue their hunches and the twinkles in their eye.
3. Do we have the right model of the process of discovery and change when we are considering how to make research "useful"? The current assumption seems to follow a linear model of a research process.

For a piece of work to be assessed as "relevant" by a funding body, it may follow a pattern something like the following: a researcher identifies a topic of interest; the case that doing work on this topic will be relevant to policy or practice will be made; those assessing the proposal will make a judgement on the basis of the scientific merit and its relevance at face value; the proposal is funded; some token users and "beneficiaries" are involved in advisory groups or in a peripheral consultative capacity; a book discussing the findings from the project will be published with a print run of a few hundred copies. Despite an acknowledgement of relevance, the research endeavour remains centrally within the academic research environment. This can perhaps be described as the weak user mode.

The Joseph Rowntree Foundation is rather slowly, and in some ways painfully, working towards a rather different model of the relationship between research and use (Lewis 1997). This is posited on the observation that research findings, in themselves, do not change anything. Findings help to illuminate the ways in which things are currently working and can provide pointers to possible changes, but need to be interpreted before they can become "useful". What is probably crucial to making research useful—to turning the findings into action—is that those who have to take the action take some *ownership* for that change and are convinced of the appropriateness of the evidence, or the argument underlying it. Findings do not have to be "relevant" in themselves to be able to bring about change. A different way of defining the problem—a paradigm shift of some kind—can come about as a result of a piece of research. A commitment to a knowledge-based society means that a premium should be put on research-based evidence, but we also know that other kinds of evidence, such as experience and practice wisdom, can be equally important levers for action.

This different conception of the research and use process, which can perhaps be called the *strong* user mode, requires a quite fundamental change in the relationship between researcher and "user". It is likely to require the user to be much more centrally involved in setting the research agenda and for identifying the focus of concern. The researcher needs to see him- or herself as a partner in the endeavour—providing skills and knowledge of the research process and the wider intellectual canvas. This can be threatening to inexperienced researchers who are struggling to establish a professional identity for themselves. They need support to be able to move in this direction. Building relations of trust between potential research "users" and researchers also takes time.

The way in which research and researchers are currently managed within the academic sector is not conducive to finding innovative ways of working with research users. There are some challenges to the way in which research is funded and managed in the academic sector if we are to find ways of making research findings useful while maintaining high scientific standards. (Interestingly, the government appears to see "knowledge transfer" as a different process from making research relevant. The *Times Higher Education Supplement* of 7 April 2000 reported that Lord Sainsbury, the science minister, considered that funding for knowledge transfer should become a permanent third stream alongside funding for teaching and research.)

The Management of Different Streams and Modes of Research

Almost all research in universities is carried out within the same management framework, which is itself an extension of the way in which universities have supported research and scholarship in earlier eras. The traditional expectation is that research and teaching need to be closely intertwined. This may well be correct for those members of staff who are on permanent teaching contracts, but it certainly does not apply to many of those carrying out research tasks who have virtually no teaching responsibilities. This includes both researchers working on contract on specific pieces of work and the increasing number of retired or early retired academics who still retain some link with their former department, probably to continue with their research interests.

A large proportion of the research being carried out in the higher education sector is funded by external bodies of some kind. The funding is usually for specific projects carried out to a specific timetable. It is expected that the work will be done quickly and to time and that staff will be skilled and experienced and not need training to enable them to do the work. The quality of the written output will also be important.

Debates about the respective roles and links between teaching and research are ongoing in many institutions, particularly the new universities. But little attention seems to be being given to the management structures and organization of contract research, in either the weak or strong user mode. A very high proportion of staff working on research projects are employed on short-term contracts. This allows little opportunity for individuals to develop their knowledge of a field or to expand and deepen their research skills. Many PhDs still provide very limited training and experience in a range of research methods and very few short-term contract researchers have the time or space for training to fill any gaps. Despite the Concordat signed by research funders and universities which outlines ways in which contract researchers should be provided with opportunities, they continue to be very low in the pecking order—far below graduate students.

Projects involving a number of staff, many quite junior, and working to tight deadlines and specifications need considerable management and support. But this also sits uneasily within traditional academic staffing structures. Recent research carried out for the Higher Education Funding Council for England (HEFCE) long-term review of research and funding has suggested that the research process has become more "managed" in response to the Research Assessment Exercises. This may well be right at the level of the university where there is greater concern about developing appropriate strategies to promote good research. But it is not clear that there is greater management of the research endeavour at the level of the research unit or team. Yet the successful completion of contract research projects, carried out within the *weak* user mode cannot be left to the mercies of mainly short-term contract staff. Developing the kinds of relationship that are needed to successfully achieve *strong* user mode research is probably altogether outside the remit of most academic institutions.

Strong user mode research depends for its success on developing links over time with the "user" and "beneficiary" communities. Many users are not experienced at thinking about or dealing with research or researchers and an education process has therefore to take place. But there is no opportunity to develop such links within an essentially project-based funding scheme which is paralleled with project-based employment of staff. Some government departments like the Department of Health have got round this difficulty by funding research units on a rolling contract basis, thus allowing relationships to develop between specific researchers and policy makers working in the same area. But most funding bodies do not have the resources to commit funds on such a basis over a long period of time. To provide the infrastructure to allow these longer-term relationships to develop and prosper requires an investment by the employing bodies, such as universities. This leads on to issues of research funding.

The Funding of Research in Higher Education Institutions

There is a continuing dilemma as to who is responsible for paying for more "relevant" research. Scholarship is legitimately seen as part of the responsibility of the higher education funding councils (although as we have seen, there appear to be fewer opportunities to get funded to do such work). In the past there has been an assumption that the funding council provided the infrastructure for research and that those who were contributing to the development of the knowledge base from outside the universities, like the research councils or charitable funders, would simply pay the marginal cost of employing staff and their expenses. This assumption was the basis for what has been called the "dual support" system.

Circumstances have changed over time, partly because of the expansion of contract research. The formal dual support system began to be unwieldy and difficult to control. There has therefore been a shift of responsibility from the Higher Education Funding Councils to the research councils, plus a transfer of funds, so that more of the infrastructure costs are now covered within research council project funding.

The shift has created an anomalous position for charitable bodies. The dual support system is said still to exist and the charities therefore continue with what was their normal practice of not meeting the indirect costs associated with the projects they funded. There is a part of the funding formula of the Higher Education Funding Councils that is meant to meet the shortfall in funds that those carrying out the research therefore experience. But many researchers and units do not appear to benefit from these funds because many of the financial transactions happen at the level of the organization. The decisions made by the vice chancellor and university finance officers may allocate funds back to the units that "earned" them or decide to subsidize some other part of their empire. Some research units have indicated that they may not be able to "afford" to put research proposals to charitable trusts because the indirect costs associated with the projects would not be covered. The role of the university, through the HEFC financial allocation, in supporting "relevant" research commissioned by external bodies appears therefore to be diminishing.

Funds for research from the private or public sectors are potentially more rewarding for researchers in that such funders pay the full cost of the research. However, the competition for such funds is often intense so that units may well bid for work at below the full cost. Given the difficulty of calculating the overhead costs of particular pieces of work, it can also sometimes be difficult to know what the full costs of such work actually are.

Research is now big business in universities and their funds are also very stretched. The funding formulae are extremely complex and difficult to understand. It seems that any small change in the formula can have disastrous financial consequences for particular institutions. There has therefore been a strong push within university administrations to find ways of controlling the variability. Universities have also been under pressure to be more accountable and the government has been seeking ways of encouraging the reward of good performance. The shift away from the block grant system of the 1960s and 1970s to a selective system linked with the assessment of research and teaching performance has been the result and is meant to provide more "accountability". But at the present time, the financial allocations that result from the RAE process are complex and lack transparency. I suspect that few outside the higher reaches of university finance

—and perhaps not all of them—understand how the system works and what impacts it has in practice. Without clarity about this it is difficult to see how the current financial arrangements are providing the expected financial incentives.

The Role and Effect of the Research Assessment Exercise

If there were such a thing as a social science "law" I suggest that one would be that "a performance *indicator* immediately becomes a performance *objective* especially if money is involved". The Research Assessment Exercise is a prime demonstration of this law. The primary measure of the quality of research, used in the RAEs, is the quality of the outputs. But this is a very limited measure of research quality in any rounded sense. Many others could be suggested, such as the kinds of criteria used to judge the quality of research proposals. These tend to include measures such as:

- clear objectives for the research (whether for exploratory/fundamental or applied work);
- methods used that are appropriate to the objectives;
- research carried out efficiently and ethically;
- data analysed imaginatively;
- results published in formats suitable to the audience, including reports accessible to a non-academic audience;
- making a genuine contribution to the development of understanding and the body of knowledge on the subject.

There are also other ways of measuring performance which are more "process"-oriented, as the TQA (Teaching Quality Assessment). To my knowledge there has been no analysis of the comparative effectiveness of the two approaches—although both are enormously expensive in time and resources. University staff have to spend many hours compiling the relevant material and completing the forms and then there is the time taken to make the assessments. The aggregate cost to the higher education sector of participating in the 1996 Research Assessment Exercise was £27.3 million (HEFCE, SHEFCE, DEFCW, DENI 1997: 2).

The focus on outputs as the key measure of research performance need not, in itself, lead to research being carried out that is not "relevant". But the particular outputs that have been included in the assessments to date have had this effect. In past assessment exercises the focus has been on articles in peer-reviewed journals and books, with different journals being rated on a hierarchy of esteem. Because of criticisms that this has undervalued particular kinds of work, such as applied and interdisciplinary studies, the 2001 RAE will be including a wider range of outputs including articles in professional and practitioner journals, published conference proceedings and research output in non-print media. The panels making the assessments are being encouraged to give parity of esteem to work from different sources. The contribution that a piece of work has made to the advance of policy and practice is also likely to be a criterion of assessment of particular pieces of work.

The next RAE will therefore be attempting to grapple more explicitly with the issue of "relevance". However, simply to include a wider range of outputs does not, in itself, solve the problem. The paradigm within which the assessment is being carried out is an "academic" one, with at best a *weak* user mode. If a researcher pursues the *strong* mode to a possible ultimate position where he or she is facilitating a research user to write the report, or to use the knowledge gained to make a significant change within an organization or take action differently, without a report being written, there would be no brownie points in the RAE. Written outputs of the kind demanded by the RAE are essentially an academic device. The whole process of journal publishing including peer review and great competition for publication means that "relevant" pieces of work can be dated before they become published.

The focus on outputs has a further, to some extent unintended, consequence. Although the unit of assessment for the RAE is the university department or equivalent, and therefore operates at an aggregate level, in practice the outputs are assessed in relation to individuals. The expectation is that all full-time research active staff should be able to cite four pieces of research output. There is therefore an assumption that each researcher is an island unto themselves, with all the skills needed to carry out and write up a piece of work. In reality, and especially in relation to applied work, this is not necessarily the case. For large-scale pieces of empirical research, working within a team of researchers is becoming the norm and such teamwork is likely to be much more effective and rewarding. Within such teams there may be people who are excellent at interviewing but hopeless at writing; people who are expert on statistics and sample design but no good at interpreting data; and people who are only mediocre researchers on their own but who are good at getting people to work together and who are crucial to the dynamics of the group. There is little opportunity to take these kinds of issues on board within the RAE, which is therefore implicitly assuming the "lone scholar" model of research.

The lack of recognition of the team approach also means that interdisciplinary work is undervalued. The notion of "disciplines" is clearly within the academic paradigm. For much applied social science, the discipline base of the researcher has become almost irrelevant. Research skills and experience develop over time. Knowledge of the issues and how to apply one's skills then becomes the key issue. There are a number of excellent social researchers who started as mathematicians or engineers. For much applied work, therefore, "disciplines" and an "interdisciplinary focus" are an irrelevance. What is at issue is whether the researchers tackling the issue have knowledge and expertise that can contribute to greater understanding of the "problem" that is being addressed. But within an academic context and from the perspective of the RAE, these situations cannot be addressed. The concern seems to be to find a way of separating projects into their constituent disciplinary parts so that they can be appropriately assessed, thus creating a form of straitjacket, or to treat "interdisciplinary" work as almost a new discipline in itself.

In the context of teamworking, any proper assessment of outputs should be taking "inputs" into account as well. As indicated earlier, the increase

9

in the number of researchers employed on short-term contracts and the expansion of project-based work puts a heavy premium on management and support, particularly for more junior members of staff. The way in which a team is managed is an important component in its success. But the management role is invisible within the RAE process—another indication of an inappropriate emphasis on individual performance. There also appear to be no incentives in the system to encourage universities to give attention to this issue, or to encourage and reward the management role. A report of work in Scotland found no sign within universities of systematic attention being paid to managing staff performance. There was no monitoring to allow an individual's performance to be quickly diagnosed and remedied. "Managers receive little or no training and their effectiveness is not monitored" (Davies 2000).

Conclusions

Social science research is rather different from much "hard" science because it studies what is all around us—the everyday—and tries to find ways of understanding it. This understanding is at a number of different levels ranging from the academic and intellectual to the person in the street—and is probably most powerful when it can link the two. The concern for the "everyday" has led in recent years to a call for social science research to be "relevant" so that it can be "useful". Such a focus is being given particular prominence by the current government, which is stressing the importance of building policy and practice from the *evidence base* and the need to assess "what works?" This paper is not the place to examine and discuss the extent to which the relevant evidence is available, or whether it is possible to successfully link the political process of policy making to the rational assessment of evidence. But the call for *relevance* continues and has implications for the way in which social science research is funded and managed.

In the "hard" sciences the concern is to make new discoveries which are then "transferred" to make new products or improve current processes. The social sciences do not usually make discoveries of this kind and the focus is more in terms of insights and ways of seeing things differently, often linked to information derived from empirical data. The preoccupation with *relevance* can lead to an emphasis on whether the focus of the information gathering and the empirical work links to a current concern, but this is to see it in a short-term and very limited way. To be truly useful and relevant a piece of work also needs to link into wider understandings and to be doing more than simply providing *information*.

Funds for social science research come from within the academic tradition of enquiry and from other funders with different purposes such as charitable foundations wishing "to do good" and government departments wanting to get answers to specific questions or to evaluate particular interventions. What is currently happening is that there is pressure on the traditional "academic" funders of research to be supporting more *relevant* work. This inevitably leads on to questions of "relevant for whom?" and the need to consider the role of potential research users and beneficiaries. Universities and research councils are not themselves in a position to define relevance, unlike those who commission research who are seeking answers to particular questions, and this has therefore to be delegated to the researchers themselves. The article argues that for research to be most relevant researchers need to build strong links with users and to work in partnership with them.

The structure within which most research is being carried out in universities has essentially changed little over time. The whole of the contract research environment has been grafted on to structures which emphasize the close relationship between teaching and research, and the importance of research as scholarship. The systematic development of knowledge based on research, as an activity in its own right, is not valued and rewarded. There are few incentives to create research teams, to nurture and develop staff within them and to manage them creatively. Nor do the structures facilitate the creation of the strong relationships with potential research users that are needed to transform the current "academic" approach to one that is genuinely seeking to carry out "relevant" work.

The whole apparatus of the Research Assessment Exercise reinforces "academic" as opposed to "relevant" research. Current arrangements do not differentiate between the different kinds of research and it is assumed that all can be managed in the same way. Yet individual scholarship and research is a very different activity from the team endeavour necessary for much contract research. By failing to recognize the conditions necessary for the range of different kinds of research, the universities, research councils and particularly the Higher Education Funding Councils are failing to provide the best environment for the different endeavours. This lack of differentiation also means little attention is being given to the need to make better connections between the intellectual, theoretical, and reflective aspects of research with the information and understandings arising from empirical work. For the research to be truly "relevant", this needs to happen.

References

Blunkett, D. (2000), *Influence or Irrelevance: Can Social Science Improve Government?*, Secretary of State's ESRC Lecture Speech, London: ESRC/DfEE.

Chancellor of the Duchy of Lancaster (1993), *Realizing Our Potential*, Cm 2250, London: HMSI.

Davies, J. K. (2000), *Improving Staff Performance in Higher Education*, Higher Education Training Organization. Quoted in *Times Higher Education Supplement*, 7 April.

HEFCE, SHEFCE, HEFCW, DENI (1997), *Research Assessment: Consultation*, London: HMSO.

Lewis, J. (1997), Promoting Change, *Search* 28, Autumn, York: Joseph Rowntree Foundation.

Scottish Higher Education Funding Council (2000), *Research and the Knowledge Age*, A Consultation Document, Edinburgh: SHEFC.

2

The Politics of Partnership in Tropical Public Health: Researching Tuberculosis Control in India

Jessica A. Ogden and
John D. H. Porter

Keywords

Partnership; Collaboration; International public health

> We live in a changing world. Relationships and roles are being redefined, as barriers are being broken down, and we are discovering new ways of working together. We now understand that vertical approaches to service delivery are inefficient, that selfish competitiveness must be replaced by a rational and equitable distribution of resources, and that collaboration creates synergism—multiplying the positive impact of our endeavours.
> (Dr Uton Muchtar Rafei, Regional Director, World Health Organization, Regional Office, in WHO 1999)

Introduction

It is in the spirit of Dr Rafei's positive ruminations on the changing nature of our world that this paper is written. In it we explore the difficulties of negotiating a productive path through the dynamics of power and control that characterize international research collaborations. We argue that the current rhetoric of "partnership" obfuscates rather than clarifies these complexities, and we call for a more open and candid debate. It is hoped that, by its inclusion in a journal on social policy, this paper may also stimulate discussion on the extent to which these issues are particular to international relationships or are, indeed, generalizable to national-level partnerships and collaborations in the UK and Europe.

The world is changing. We are becoming more "globalized" and this entails a rethinking of the kinds of relationships being created to research and intervene in international health. In many ways, however, "globalization" is dividing us rather than bringing us together (Lee 1999). It has been argued, for example, that globalization is serving to increase the divide

Figure 1

Flow of information and expertise as a linear process

(Evidence on which to base "best practice")

Development of international policy

Development (and financing) of national policy and programmes

National policy/Programmes devolve to districts

Delivery of services to the community

between rich and poor countries, between the post-industrialized countries of the "North", and the still industrializing countries of the "South", not least in terms of burden of disease (Lee 1999). This is the context, then, for the recent entrée of the notions of "collaboration" and "partnership" into the world of international health. On the one hand there is an understanding that there is a need to be involved in relationships which will bridge differences and synergistically lead to interventions that go wider than mere competitive interests (WHO 1999). On the other hand, however, it is not clear that we have as yet discovered how to create these synergistic relationships. It appears instead that the usual flow of information and expertise continues to run from the international, through the national to the local levels, as depicted in the solid arrows in figure 1.

Yet, through the work we have been doing on tuberculosis in India and Africa, it has become increasingly clear that this model does not foster the creation of effective policy. Our intention is to be involved in a paradigm shift in international public health whereby the flow can be reversed— or rather that a parallel flow of information, knowledge and expertise can proceed "upwards" through the levels, enabling international policy to be informed by local situations—as shown in the dashed arrows in figure 1. This process entails the development of different kinds of relationships, different relationships of power (or more conscious understandings of the importance of power in structuring relationships) and differently oriented displays of respect (Ogden 2000; Ogden and Porter 1999; Porter *et al.* 1999a; 1999b).

What is normally meant by partnership in the context of international research? A number of attempts at definition have been made. Pearson (1969), in an earlier context, writes that "partnership entails the need to specify reciprocal rights and obligations and to establish clear objectives that are beneficial to both parties." A more current account holds that the essence of partnership is "a relationship based upon agreement, reflecting mutual responsibilities in furtherance of shared interests" (OECD/DAC 1996). Partnership in the health sector has been described by WHO as a process of bringing together "a set of actors for the common goal of improving the health of populations based on mutually agreed roles and principles" (Kickbusch and Quick 1998). These definitions take us some way towards understanding the principles underlying the development of partnerships, but they do not take adequate account of the politics of relationship. Thus the principles they outline are difficult to envision and to realize in everyday practice.

In this paper we interrogate the language of partnership through the example of two international research collaborations in which we have been involved. Our purpose here is to understand something about the politics of international research collaborations in order that we may do them better—even if doing them better means nothing more than being willing to problematize the whole notion of "partnership" and our engagement with it. We ask whether these themes are present also in other sectors and other contexts, and invite discussion in order to move the debate, and the substantive issues around which that debate revolves, forward.

This paper recounts the unfolding of two related international research collaborations. Both were operational research projects, instigated and funded by the Overseas Development Administration (ODA),[1] now called the Department for International Development, UK (DFID), in the Spring of 1996. Both were international collaborations between Indian research institutions and the London School of Hygiene and Tropical Medicine. We argue that attaining partnership between Northern and Southern research institutes, in the sense described in the rhetoric (cited above), itself needs to be a shared objective, and that it can be easily and swiftly undermined by conflicting (even if tacit) agendas. The creation of research partnerships is further undermined by global economic structures that create the illusion of an unequal distribution of expertise—higher salary and institutional costs in the North might suggest, for example, greater academic expertise, which then has to be justified in joint research proposals. We suggest that while the rhetoric and intention of North/South research partnerships in international public health are important, they do not, yet, effectively deal with or manage the real issues of power and control which underlie much work in international public health and which continue to characterize relationships between the North and South.

The evidence on which we base this exposition is not firm. The documentary data we rely on are almost entirely the correspondence between the various institutions involved. The remainder of the data consist mainly of our own memories, experiences and, indeed, feelings of the events and experiences recounted. After discussing and defining terms, we give a brief overview of tuberculosis and relevant developments in tuberculosis policy in India, which led to the creation of the terms of reference, by the ODA, for the collaborative research projects undertaken. We then undertake to illustrate key developments in the collaborations and partnerships that ensued and unveil the nature of our own agendas. We conclude by returning to the tentative framework proposed in figure 2.

Figure 2

Framework for partnership and collaboration

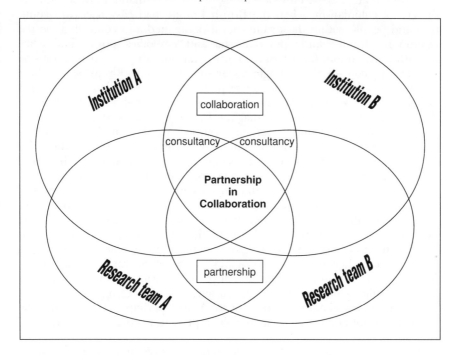

Terminology of Relationship

It emerges from this story that it is important to make a distinction between the partnerships developed between institutions for the purposes of research, and those made between the individuals involved, and that this distinction may be important enough to warrant a semantic separation. Thus we offer the tentative suggestion that the former be referred to as "collaborations" and the latter as "partnerships". This semantic separation is intended to call attention to the differences in power between institutions and people, and the differences in the types of relationship made between institutions and people. A third type of relationship referred to here is "consultancy". The term "consultancy" implies that a person works for an organization for a period of time, and during that time works to the agenda of that organization. It is thus according to standard usage that we refer to consultancy in this paper, while we propose a rethinking of the ways in which "collaboration" and "partnership" have come to be understood in the policy literature. It is by inverting the usual ways in which these terms are used that we attempt to call attention to the jargon, and to stimulate self-consciousness in its use. These relationships are represented schematically in figure 2.

Institutions can be key symbols of power. This power is as much about history as about the present. The London School of Hygiene and Tropical

Jessica A. Ogden and John D. H. Porter

Medicine, for example, which celebrated its centenary in 1999, has a long and distinguished history. Many important advances in tropical medicine have been made here. Many of these advances were made, however, during the era of colonialism, when the British Empire had easy access to countries and people within those countries it dominated and controlled. So the institution—its name and reputation—has and "embodies" power. It also, like any other institution, has rules, structures and procedures, which lie outside the personal control of any single researcher working within its walls. These two factors—the symbolic and active power of the institution plus its rules and structures—are central to the creation of international research collaborations. It is not necessarily vital that the two or more *institutions* involved in collaboration share values, goals and purposes, although this would certainly support the relationship. The moral element to the relationship, then, is largely left to the human beings—the individual researchers and administrators—to work out. The essence of "partnership" lies in this realm.

This is not to say, however, that the residue of institutional power and symbolism do not play a part in the creation of partnerships between researchers in international collaborations. These may feature strongly in the decisions made about specific roles, commitments and inputs of the various actors. They may also flavour the kind of demeanour assumed by individuals towards each other, for example displays, or not, of deference or superiority. Yet these aspects of the collaboration dovetail also with the small "p" politics of partnership: issues of gender, status, age, ethnicity/caste, etc. will affect the nature of the relationships developed. As will, perhaps most crucially, the existence or not of a common set of values, priorities and goals, underpinned by respect.

This story is about research partnerships, not tuberculosis (TB). However some background information on TB might be useful to enable readers from other disciplines to more fully understand the context in which the story takes place.

Tuberculosis

Tuberculosis is estimated to be responsible for 2 to 3 million deaths annually, including at least 100,000 children, in whom—after malaria, acute respiratory and gastrointestinal disease—it is a leading cause of mortality. Amongst infectious agents, tuberculosis is the single most important cause of adult death (Grange 1999). Because of the interaction between tuberculosis and HIV infection, the effect of the HIV/AIDS pandemic on tuberculosis has been devastating. In 1996, the number of people estimated to be infected with both HIV and TB was over 6 million (WHO 1996), with the majority living in sub-Saharan Africa.

Tuberculosis is a disease intimately associated with social and economic conditions. It is said to be a disease of development: "a barometer of social justice and equity" (Ogden *et al.* 1999). Increasing numbers of TB cases began to be reported in western industrialized countries in the late 1980s, but TB has continued to be a major health problem in developing countries throughout the past century, principally because of poverty (e.g. Spence *et al.*

16

1993; Stephens 1999). Countries like India report between 2.5 and 3 million new cases each year with 0.3 to 0.5 million deaths (Chakraborty 1997). It is a disease which reflects the international gulf between the North and the South and the increasing gap between the rich and poor in all countries: a theme reflected in publications on globalization where some writers have argued that the process of globalization is leading to increased marginalization of certain groups (Lee 1999).

The DFID tuberculosis programme

In 1994, to help address international research, training and capacity building in TB, the ODA developed Terms of Reference for institutions to bid for funds for a "Tuberculosis Research Programme, 1995–2000". The competitive bid was won by the London School of Hygiene and Tropical Medicine and the Nuffield Institute for Health in Leeds.

The purpose of the research programme is "to conduct relevant research which influences global and national TB control policies, promoting the appropriate use of resources for the reduction of tuberculosis morbidity and mortality". Work is concentrated in sub-Saharan Africa, and in India, Pakistan and Nepal. The programme provides salaries for UK-based researchers to conduct work with collaborators overseas. An essential part of the programme is to develop collaborations with overseas institutions and to be involved in training.

A major piece of programme work was conducted in India between 1995 and 1999. This work involved researchers from a variety of disciplines (anthropology, epidemiology, medicine, health policy) and focused on issues of TB programme implementation. An essential part of the work involved the development of collaborations and partnerships with a variety of Indian organizations and researchers.

Tuberculosis in India and the Revised National Tuberculosis Programme

India today carries the heaviest burden of tuberculosis in the world. The estimated number of infections, indicated above, is staggering. It is thus ironic that India has had a National Tuberculosis Programme (NTP) since the 1960s. At the time of its creation it was one of the most evidence-based and effective programmes in the world (Rangan *et al.* 1997; Banerji 1993). In 1992, however, as tuberculosis was rapidly rising on the international health agenda, the NTP came under external audit (WHO 1992). The evaluation team, which included international tuberculosis experts from the World Health Organization (WHO), the International Union Against Tuberculosis and Lung Disease (IUATLD) and the Swedish International Development Agency (SIDA), as well as Indian members, found that the NTP was not performing well. They found that too few people were being cured (only 35 per cent), that drug supplies were erratic, the quality of the laboratory diagnosis techniques was not uniformly good, and so on. It was thus decided that India should revise its national programme in accordance with WHO guidelines for TB control. Most of the funding would come from a World Bank loan to the government of India, with bilateral donors (notably ODA and DANIDA, the Danish International Development Agency) supporting the process in a number of specified sites. ODA undertook to support two sites in Delhi and the district of Medak in Andhra Pradesh, making clear that a condition of their support would be relative autonomy in the way in which the pilots would be carried out in these sites. ODA were particularly concerned that they be able to conduct operational research to determine the effectiveness of the new system, and that the programme would reach and meet the needs of the most vulnerable members of these populations.

Terms of Reference for the Operations Research

Thus, in April 1996 ODA issued its terms of reference for the operational research to be carried out in these three sites. It was anticipated that the results from the research would be immediately useful to programmers and policy makers responsible for scaling up the Revised National Tuberculosis Control Programme (RNTCP). These terms were sent out to a number of Indian and international research institutions and researchers, and one of the stipulations of the funding was that any *"international agency bidding for the funds must have a local partner institute to work with"*. Enclosed with the Terms of Reference was a list of names and addresses of everyone who had been sent them. There were two parts to the list; one headed INDIA, under which were listed all the Indian individuals/institutions invited to submit proposals, and one headed EUROPE under which were listed all European individuals/institutions who had been invited to submit. Thirteen names/addresses were listed under each rubric.

While the need for the international groups to have Indian collaborators was made explicit in these terms of reference, a corresponding need for the Indian groups was not stated. This is an increasingly common element of proposals of this kind. The implicit expectation, that the Indians do collaborate with overseas groups, may be based on any number of assumptions. For example, as a bilateral donor, ODA may expect that British researchers be involved, and that the Indian groups would benefit from the collaboration through capacity building. On the Indian side it may be expected that links to a reputable British research institution would increase the likelihood of obtaining the funding. In any case, however, an effect of this approach is that we in London needed them more than they needed us.

The purpose of the research being commissioned was to improve the implementation of the RNTCP in the three ODA-supported sites. It was also hoped that the projects would aid the development of the RNTCP at national level. The projects were expected to contribute to ODA's priorities of increasing TB control coverage to 70 per cent of the population, to ensure 85 per cent of infectious cases were cured, and to aid the scaling up of projects from pilot to state level.

As for content, there were four main subject areas around which they were seeking proposals. These were (1) to assess the TB treatment needs of the population; (2) to explore perceptions and understandings of TB in these areas; (3) to explore the range and type of health care providers in the areas treating TB, and how these providers are used by people in obtaining care; (4) to look for ways to bring private and other non-governmental providers into the programme to increase its reach and coverage of the population. It was also expected that the research would make recommendations for the development of key health systems required for RNTCP expansion within the state and improve organizational arrangements.

Developing the "Collaborations"

Three researchers at the London School—two within the ODA TB Programme (the authors, Porter and Ogden) and one in the Department of Public Health and Policy—received the terms of reference. We agreed it was important to respond to the call for letters of intent, but we were unsure about which of the possible Indian researchers identified on the list to approach about collaboration. We contacted a colleague in the ODA office in Delhi for some suggestions, and he suggested we approach Dr A at a social service training institute in Andhra Pradesh, and Dr B at a tuberculosis hospital and research institute in Delhi. Dr A himself is a physician who moved out of clinical medicine and into research. He and his team had some background and experience carrying out programme-related operational research, although not the kind of qualitative work envisaged for these projects. Dr B was a practising chest physician, whose team did not have previous social science research experience. Shortly after this, one of the London team, a social anthropologist, had the opportunity to meet with Dr B and his team in Delhi. Although they had not yet been sent the terms of reference (they were not on the original list), they were glad to be involved. Their hospital had recently been granted the status of a research institute by the government, and they were keen to begin research activities of this kind. They were also quite interested in learning more about qualitative research methods for TB control.

Back in London, a team was assembled to discuss the terms of reference and to draft letters of intent. These were sent out to Drs A and B, together with a request for collaboration. As a part of this request we suggested including in the collaboration an NGO, based in Mumbai, with which we had worked, and which had extensive experience in conducting qualitative research of this kind on tuberculosis. Both parties responded positively and eventually letters of intent were sent to ODA directly from the Indian institutes in early June. The London team was included in the letters of intent as collaborators, but did not see the final drafts of the letters before they were sent.

In late July we received word, via our collaborators, that ODA had asked us to submit full proposals for both projects. Some discussion ensued regarding the substantive content of the proposals, but the main issues that arose were to do with the nature of the research collaboration and the content of our respective roles in the research process.

On 14 August we received communications from both groups, and perceived a significant shift in the tenor of their correspondence as well as important changes to the content of the proposals themselves. Prior to this time ODA had convened a meeting in Hyderabad of all Indian researchers who had been shortlisted for the operations research, to coordinate and discuss key substantive and administrative issues. The deadline for submission of final proposals was 16 August, so there was also a sense of urgency in these letters. Both letters stipulated the expected nature of the London group's role in the research process, and requested that we send the appropriate budget forms to them as soon as possible. Below are excerpts from these letters:

Offer from Dr A

"We are proposing to use tools like focus groups, in-depth interviews and PRA [Participatory Rural Appraisal] techniques for collecting the data. While we do have expertise available in these areas, we feel that we could immensely benefit from your experience. We, therefore, request you to join our team as a *consultant* providing these specific inputs. We feel that this will involve two trips to India each covering 15 days, one for development of tools and another during analysis. Probably you may also need some additional time in London for preparation. If you are interested please do send me the confirmation indicating your consultancy fee and travel costs." (emphasis added)

Offer from Dr B

The Delhi group were less explicit, and offered us a choice of collaborative arrangements:

"We are enclosing a brief of the renewed proposal plan for the operational research study in Delhi. We feel that your expertise in the field of Anthropology will be of great help to us in designing our research tools and also during the analysis of the qualitative data we intend to collect for this study. In the event that you are still interested in collaborating with our project I would request you to kindly send the requisite information . . . as required by ODA, or else we can offer you a consultancy for providing about four weeks support to the study. I would appreciate if you could indicate your decision at the earliest by fax."

Our response

In both cases our response was to write letters indicating that we wanted the research to represent *collaborations* and *partnerships* rather than consultancies. Our intention and hope from the outset of the project, as communicated to both groups, was to be research *partners* rather than technical consultants. We stated that we had been looking forward to the operations research as an opportunity for initiating long-term collaborations. We noted the problem of disparities in costs between our institutions, and explained that consultancies are far more expensive than collaborations. We sent two alternative costings, one reflecting the 40-day consultancy (£18,000), and the other a 14-month collaboration with the TB Programme: 15% of Ogden's time over 14 months;

15% for administrative support over 14 months, and Porter's participation gratis (£16,500). An excerpt from our response to Dr A is reproduced below:

We are anxious to stress that our interest is in developing long-term collaborations with your institution rather than links through consultancies. The intention of the TB Programme is to be involved in substantive collaborations with Indian research institutions interested in tuberculosis control in India. We do not feel that a consultancy role enables full use to be made of the resources and skills available here, nor will consultancy satisfactorily meet our own research priorities and objectives.

You may feel that, given the specific circumstances of this project, consultancy is the best or most realistic way to fund collaboration at this time. If this is the case, then we would be willing to proceed on the basis that together we understand the consultancy as a step on the way to true collaborations in the future. Please do let us know how you would like to proceed.

Both groups were quick to respond to our concerns.

Reply from Dr A

"We are certainly keen to establish a long-term relationship with your institute and we are looking forward for institutional tie-up with this project. Due to changed outlook of the project, I myself was not sure what support we could ask from your team and since anthropological approach would be the mainstay we thought we could justify your [Ogden's] participation. As the deadline was short, during the workshop it was in principle agreed that we could enlist other collaborators of the study (the Mumbai-based NGO) as consultants to save from formalities. This in no way means to undermine their role and made essentially to overcome the technical issues of justification and meeting the deadline of 16th August. I do hope that I have made our position clear. Please do feel free to suggest if you need any modifications or additions. I could discuss with our team and get back to you."

Reply from Dr B

"Please find enclosed the proposed draft proposal which we intend to submit to ODA. I appreciate your strong sentiments regarding the project and hope you will understand our predicaments and constraints too. At present we are suggesting full-time collaboration with your institute. In case the budgetary constraints force ODA to suggest a consultative arrangement, we shall discuss and decide. We will always welcome any opportunity to work with Dr Porter, you and your team. Kindly go through the draft proposal and return at the earliest with your comments."

Through this process, therefore, we managed to develop a common under-standing of what the nature and content of the *collaborations* would be. Note, however, that *partnership* has not yet had time to develop. This was to happen at a later stage, as we began to work together on the projects.

Developing "Partnerships"

In October 1996 we were informed that both proposals had been accepted. Following the awarding of the contracts, the different teams of researchers came together on several occasions in Delhi; to plan the research; develop the methodologies and tools; to review the work, and finally to conduct an evaluation and to write up the project. Both projects were run from the Indian institutes, and they conducted the fieldwork. There were, however, from our perspective, qualitative differences in the nature of the collabora-tions with the two groups.

Our experience in Andhra Pradesh was that the relationship did not move beyond the original suggestion for "consultancy", although the institutional arrangement was for collaboration. Power dynamics played a key role. The impression in London was that while the symbolic power of the London School, as an institution, was helpful in terms of instigating an interest in collaboration by the Indian group and remained important in terms of legit-imacy for the project, the active power was very much situated in Andhra Pradesh. Our perception was that the London group was perceived to be largely redundant. The language of collaboration and partnership "agreed" in the letters early on was not followed through. Indeed, a further layer of power and hierarchy came into play in the dynamic between Dr A and the anthropologist from London, which served to override the relative degrees of symbolic power between the institutions: Ogden, a woman, is junior to Dr A, and comes from an academic discipline with relatively low status in India. These factors served to further unseat the possibility for "partnership", as Ogden's participation on the project became increasingly marginalized. Lack of shared orientations, values and priorities were certainly apparent, and the expectation was that London would work to the agenda of Andhra Pradesh. Thus this relationship was a collaboration in institutional terms, but was a consultancy, rather than a partnership, in relationship terms.

In Delhi the experience was different. From our perspective the Delhi team appeared to carry the notion of us as full collaborators (what we are now calling "partnership") throughout the process. Working together on the research, we from London felt we were members of the team; we were kept informed of developments in the research and we were expected to muck in with the others to work through problems as they arose. The process in the Andhra Pradesh (AP) project, however, was qualitatively different. It was as if the AP team really considered us as "consultants" right the way through— as far as the institutions were concerned (the structures, and rules) we were "full collaborators", but the "partnership" never developed.

So what does this anecdote suggest about the politics of international research collaborations? In order to answer this question it is first relevant to highlight the "agendas" which underlay our interests in engaging in the collaborations, and this we do below.

Our agenda

Our agenda was to create research *partnerships* (rather than consultancies) with Indian institutions for two main reasons.

(1)   *To engender new ways forward in public health research and policy.*   It was and is our belief that part of the process of creating a shift in orientation in public health will be to change the way we perceive and engage in collaboration. This was part of the intention of encouraging and facilitating the participation in the projects of the Mumbai-based NGO. Collaborations between institutions in different states within India is rare, but it makes sense, both logistically and ideologically, to generate links of this kind. The next point relates directly to this one.

(2)   *To be able to work in partnership with skilled and knowledgeable colleagues in order to build* each other's *capacity and to contribute more substantively to improving access of patients to TB care in these settings and in India more generally.*   The people with whom we wanted to work were themselves experts in the field—if not of social science research, certainly of tuberculosis. The AP group had expertise in both areas. Being Indian, they also were in a position to know and understand the local cultures, social structures and ways of working. Thus we could not necessarily add new skills (although in both cases some methodological support was necessary from both LSHTM and the Mumbai NGO), but we considered the possibility that our participation would add to the critical mass of expertise involved on the project. From an anthropological perspective our position as "outsiders" could add an important dimension in itself: coming to a situation or problem with relatively fresh eyes can lead one to ask new questions. Some of these questions will be irrelevant (many will be ridiculous) but one or two might be useful in shifting a process further along or in revealing a new way to see and understand the problem/situation. Our relatively easy access to the international scholarly press also presented an opportunity for the wider dissemination of research results.

But to work as equal partners in the research process was/is problematic due to huge disparities in research costs between our respective institutions: LSHTM budgets work out to be between 5 and 10 times higher than Indian institution budgets—even for those charging overheads (such as the AP group). It is apparent, then, that the global structures of inequality are replicated in our professional structures. These inequalities add to the political difficulties in redressing the situation: wanting to work as equal partners, out of respect for and realization of the integrity and considerable expertise of partners, is made more difficult, if not impossible, by globalized economic structures which create an artificial, but nevertheless powerful, illusion of imbalance. Because we cost more it appears we should be *worth* more. The sensible effect of this situation is that our participation has to be justified on the specific items we are able to contribute, and that our participation needs to be kept to a minimum. But this creates an artificial image of the outsiders (from the North) being the experts and the insiders (from the South) being in need of "capacity building". It also leads to the creation of "consultancies" rather than "partnerships", and this works against the mood so eloquently set by Dr Rafei's comments quoted at the beginning of this paper.

We also had a more mundane—although not entirely unrelated—agenda, which was to create strong research partnerships with Indian institutions which could form the basis for ongoing research over the lifetime of the RNTCP pilot projects and, indeed, for the life of the TB Programme. While this would serve the function of keeping us in work, however, we were also hoping that this work would form a strong precedent for the inclusion of operational research in the RNTCP nationally, which in turn would lead to the improved effectiveness of the programme by facilitating the kind of "bottom-up" policy learning depicted in figure 1.

Naturally our collaborators also had agendas, and uncovering the nature of these would be a valuable endeavour but would require further research. We do know, however, at least some of the issues involved from the point of view of our funding body, the ODA.

While we do not yet have specific data exploring this, it is true that at the time of the operations research, the ODA were in the process of reorganiza-tion—themselves shifting the centre of working from London to the field offices overseas. As they were creating Health and Population Field Offices, so they were creating a structure and process for shifting more and more responsibility for managing research to specialist Indian research officers hired to work at ODA for this purpose.

Conclusion

In today's globalizing world the concept of "partnership" is fast becoming jargon. At the same time, however, the nature of relationships between North and South must change and is changing to account for the closing gap in capacity to carry out research of international standard. The development of a lexicon sophisticated enough to adequately address these changing relationships, however, lags behind and is not supported by the mindless recourse to the jargon of "partnership". In this paper we have tried to call attention to this complexity through recounting the story, or part of the story, of the development of two quite different, but related, international research relationships. It is hoped that by standing the jargon on its head we might call attention to it and thus force the opening up of the debate around the changing nature of research "partnerships". We suggest that there is an important difference between those aspects of the relationship that respond to institutional needs and agendas and those aspects that relate more dir-ectly to the human relationships upon which the work in the field actually depends. We set out this difference in figure 2, where the relationship between researchers is labelled "partnership" (using the word as it might be used in everyday parlance to describe a close relationship), and the institutional rela-tionship as "collaboration".

This framework is as yet preliminary and does not adequately take account of the important impact that power differentials have on all aspects of these relationships. It is hoped that the framework may be developed further as the debate opens out, and we actively encourage colleagues from the North and South to engage with us in this effort.

Acknowledgements

The authors would like to acknowledge the essential role of the Department for International Development, UK, in helping to create the development of international collaborations and partnerships. We also wish to extend thanks to all of our Indian partners from whom we have learned so much.

Note

1. Throughout this paper, when writing in a historical context, we use the old assignation, ODA, to refer to this department rather than the new one, DFID. This is in order to reflect the actors involved as accurately as possible. In the paper ODA also refers generally to the Health and Population field office in New Delhi unless otherwise indicated.

References

Banerji, D. (1993), A social science approach to strengthening India's National Tuberculosis Programme, *Ind J Tub*, 40, 2: 61–81.

Chakraborty A. K. (1997), *Prevalence and Incidence of TB Infection and Disease in India: a Comprehensive Review*, WHO/TB/97.231, Geneva: WHO.

Grange J. M. (1999), The global burden of tuberculosis. In J. D. H. Porter and J. M. Grange (eds), *Tuberculosis—an Interdisciplinary Perspective*, London: Imperial College Press, pp. 3–31.

Kickbusch, I., and Quick, J. (1998), Partnerships for health in the 21st century, *World Health Statistics Quarterly*, 51, 1: 68–74.

Lee, K. (1999), Globalization, communicable disease and equity: a look back and forth, *Development*, 42, 4, *Poverty, Health and Sustainable Development*: 35–9.

OECD/DAC (1996), *Shaping the 21st Century: The Contribution of Development Co-operation*, Paris: OECD.

Ogden, J., and Porter, J. (1999), Leprosy: applying qualitative techniques to research and intervention, *Lepr Rev*, 70: 129–35.

Ogden, J. A. (2000), Improving tuberculosis control: social science inputs, *Transactions of the Royal Society of Tropical Medicine and Hygiene*, 94: 135–40.

Ogden, J. A., Rangan, S., Uplekar, M., Porter, J., Brugha, R., Zwi, A., and Nyheim, D. (1999), Shifting the paradigm in tuberculosis control: illustrations from India, *Int J Tuberc Lung Dis.*, 3, 10: 855–61.

Pearson, L. B. (1969), *Partners in Development: Report of the Commission on International Development*, London: Commission on International Development.

Porter, J., Ogden, J., and Pronyk, P. (1999a), Infectious disease policy: towards the production of health, *Health Policy & Planning*, 14, 4: 322–8.

Porter, J., Ogden, J., and Pronyk, P. (1999b), The way forward: an integrated approach to tuberculosis control. In J. D. H. Porter and J. M. Grange (eds), *Tuberculosis: An Interdisciplinary Perspective*, London: Imperial College Press, pp. 359–78.

Jessica A. Ogden and John D. H. Porter

Rangan, S., Uplekar, M., Brugha, R., Nyheim, D., Ogden, J., Porter, J., and Zwi, A. (1997), *Tuberculosis control in India: a state of the art review*, Delhi: Department for International Development.

Spence, D. P. S., Hotchkiss, J., Williams, C. S. D., and Davies, P. D. O. (1993), Tuberculosis and poverty, *Br Med J*, 307: 759–61.

Stephens, C. (1999), The Owl and the Pussycat Went to Sea: moving towards intersectoral policies to prevent the unequal distribution of tuberculosis. In J. D. H. Porter and J. M. Grange (eds), *Tuberculosis: An Interdisciplinary Perspective*, London: Imperial College Press.

World Health Organization (1992), *Tuberculosis Programme Review, India*, Geneva: World Health Organization, September.

World Health Organization (1996), *Tuberculosis in the era of HIV. A deadly partnership*, WHO/TB/96.204, Geneva: World Health Organization.

World Health Organization (1999), *NGOs and TB Control: principles and examples for organizations joining the fight against TB*, SA/TB/213, Geneva: WHO.

3

Recognizing Diversity and Group Processes in International, Collaborative Research Work: A Case Study

Elizabeth Ettorre

Keywords

Research collaboration; Group work; Research management; International research; Cultural diversity

Introduction

In July 1998, a colleague sent me the Call for papers on "The business of research: issues of politics and practice" for this volume. I read that the object was "to offer relevant academics an opportunity to report on some of the realities of engaging in research and consultancy, in the light of their own experience". This call struck a chord in me given that I had recently completed my work as project coordinator of a large EU-funded project[1] and am currently on the Steering Group of another EU project. Therefore, I felt and still feel I have a valuable contribution to make to this volume. I find it refreshing to reflect on these international research experiences.

I started doing international, collaborative research in London in 1990. However, it was in 1996, when I was living abroad, that I made the decision to enter into research management on a European level. At that time, I believed that most if not all senior researchers who have national or world-wide prominence can "successfully" manage international, collaborative research. With hindsight, I see that my belief was based on myth, although I think this myth is "alive and well" in the academy today. Many researchers, including my "former" self, suppose that good research management is acquired through a process of trial and error and demands little thought, skill or training. It is almost as if being a good leader is a skill that one acquires as one moves up the academic hierarchy. The aim of my paper is threefold: to break the "senior academic = good leader" myth; to challenge some of the ideas surrounding it; and to establish various benchmarks for good research management, particularly on an international level.

Elizabeth Ettorre

My paper is based on the premise that successful, high-quality research management by social scientists is a resource that demands sensitivity to diversity and an awareness of group processes in a scientific context. This assumption is related to two claims: that globalization relates to intellectual processes as well as economic ones and that social science is science (that is, the proliferation of "social" into the realm of scientific knowledge is possible and commendable). First, there is growing evidence to suggest that social scientific research is becoming more global (Wallerstein 1999; Mayor 1992). Social scientists are doing more work with respect to "world formation" and this work has implications for the general everyday understanding of the contemporary world as a whole (Robertson and Khondker 1998). Second, given that the boundaries between the social and natural sciences are relaxing, it is possible to see more clearly than ever before social science as a science of the social world (Williams 2000).

Given the above premise, being sensitive to diversity means that issues such as language, race, ethnicity, nationality, gender, disability, class, age and academic status should not only inform our research findings but also guide our research practice in collaborative research settings on international levels. Any project coordinator or leader of an international research project learns fairly swiftly that diversity, or rather openness to diversity, is the name of the game.

A leader may also maintain openness to diversity for him/herself and the research group by generating an awareness of the complexities of groups and group processes. This is another essential component of this type of research management and practice. Simply, to be a good research manager and collaborator in an international setting requires knowledge of how people work in groups.

With the above issues in mind, I plan to discuss five interrelated themes in this paper: (1) setting the scene: constructing a "manageable" research package; (2) awareness of diversity as the heart of international research; (3) international research work as group work: the dynamics of research and processual issues; (4) troubleshooting; and (5) sensing the effects of research organizations and topics. Before establishing various benchmarks for good research management and practice, particularly on an international level, I would like to describe Project 96 and position it within a research context.

Setting the Scene: Constructing a "Manageable" Research Package

Gathering the "great" and the "good"

As one can imagine, much preparation work goes into planning an international research project. Initially for Project 96, a core group of senior and junior researchers had been set up by Country 1.[2] The full application to the Commission had taken at least a year to put together (from December 1993 to January 1995), while proposal writing included three months of solid writing (from January 1995 to March 1995). Gathering partners was a collective task and done through already-established networks of European researchers. Each member of the initial core group spoke to key European contacts and reported back to the group during a series of meetings. I knew it was important to target countries from southern Europe and I set that as my basic task during this preparatory time. Other members of the core group concentrated on gathering colleagues from northern Europe. We approached many colleagues and we told them about our project as well as our need for more partners. We set the limit at seven partners because we thought three partners from the originating country (Country 1) and four from three other European countries would be sufficient to mount a project and carry out the work.

In this process of gathering partners, I myself tended to follow my intuition. If I were to do it again, I would most definitely use my intuition but also try to get as much information as possible about a potential, but unknown partner who I had not worked with previously. I would do this *before* I would ask him/her to become a research partner. Rather than inviting him/her on the project on the basis of another European colleague's verbal recommendation, I would try to ensure that any information about a potential partner was based on actual knowledge of working with them in a team context. To receive a verbal recommendation from at least two colleagues who had worked with the person in a collaborative setting would be ideal. In this way, I would have a clear idea of what to expect from a partner.

Also, I would ask potential partners direct questions—questions that may be uncomfortable and which I did not ask partners in my earlier searches. For example, do you enjoy doing research with others? Are you able to listen to others in a research group? Are you able to accept a research group's decision even if it may be different from your own? Is the success of a research group as important as your own success as an academic? Are you able to share your academic work in a collective context? I would ask all of these questions with the knowledge that some academics are just not team players, for in my view, being a team player is essential in international collaborative research.

The issue of project coordination

It is essential that before any project begins, the issue of project coordination be clear between all of the involved partners. Officials in Brussels demand that one person, the project coordinator (PC), be responsible for the project. This is the case no matter how you choose to set up your project management structure.

In Project 96, some partners were not aware of the legalities involved in an EU project. That the research was based on a legal contract, designating one person within one institution as the main contractor who was legally accountable to Brussels was alien to them. Related to this, some partners, particularly those who were orientated towards a loose working structure, believed that a diffusion of power to all partners and junior researchers was more acceptable than what they saw as a hierarchical structure with a PC as leader.

While they had agreed that I was the PC as stated on the EU application, difficulties arose for them when I actually took up my leadership role. Simply, they wanted me to share the project coordination with them and be PC "in name only". Although I had every confidence in my colleagues' research skills, I disagreed with them. I believed (and still believe) quite strongly that without clear leadership from the beginning any international collaborative research project has a very good chance of failure. As PC, I was in a difficult position. On the one hand, I believed in the worth of an informal, non-hierarchical power structure, as my colleagues did. On the other hand, I had not yet worked with some of my partners and felt there needed to be a type of apprenticeship period to test their research commitments. Also, I was acutely aware that as PC I was legally responsible for the project.

I also believed (and still believe) that it would be unfair to be PC in name only and to share the PC role with a small group of partners. I wanted all partners to begin the project on an equal footing. The suggestion for the formation of a small "management clique" would be destructive and this type of management structure was contrary to the type of structure agreed in the EU contract.

The need for a consortium agreement

As a result of the above difficulty, I set up a consortium agreement (CA) which all partners signed. It stated that the project was to be led by the PC with advice from the Project Coordinating Committee (PCC) (that is, those senior partners who had signed the contract and were responsible for doing the work). Most importantly, this research agreement stated that all of the partners had an equal voice (that is, one vote on the PCC) in the research organization and execution. This emphasized that in order for the project to be successful it was essential that all partners be equal and that there would be a clear management structure. However, a tension between those who wanted an informal power structure (i.e. diffusion of power) and those who wanted a formal power structure (i.e. delegation of power) lasted for the duration of the project.

For example, during the first year of the project, some partners asked me as the PC for special consideration with regard to timetabling, their basic tasks, and the allocation of their resources. While I tended to be firm and deny these special considerations on the grounds that all partners should be treated equally, my strategy of fairness did not win their constant collegiality. Indeed it caused some tensions and at times, affected the dynamics of the entire group. These tensions became clear particularly at the annual project meetings when timetabling issues, basic tasks and allocation of resources were outlined or re-assessed within the group.

Allocation of basic research tasks

Besides the PC (Partner 1), Project 96 included 7 senior partners from four different countries: Partners 1, 2 and 3 from Country 1; Partners 4 and 5 from Country 2; Partner 6 from Country 3 and Partner 7 from Country 4. The Programme itself included a series of seven linked studies: an extensive literature review of the popular press and professional journals including a review of ethical and legal codes (Study A); surveys of key players (Studies B, C, D, Ea and Ec) and one country-specific population study (Study Eb). The work was structured in such a way that each study including the organization of basic tasks would be headed by a senior researcher. The project management structure is outlined in table 1 and this was included in Annex II[3] to the contract under "Coordination and organization". This section of the contract stated that the role of the PC would be to ensure the "network style" of working amongst the multidisciplinary researcher partners. Besides overall coordination, I was to facilitate the exchange of information amongst research partners; keep on hand all updated progress reports from research partners; organize this information into a research project archive and distribute it when required. This section of the Annex also mentioned that a PCC had been established; that research partners and their project tasks were outlined in table 1 and that the tasks of junior scientific and technical personnel were also included in the table.

The allocation of basic tasks as listed in table 1 did not always work out in practice. This happened in two areas: coordination of specific projects and organization of timetables. Those partners who wanted a diffuse, informal power structure tended to delegate their tasks to junior colleagues in their specific institutions. These junior colleagues were very competent, but at times there was lack of clarity on the direction of the research projects which had been delegated. In this respect, it is very important for PCs to ensure that while some senior partners may have very busy schedules, they must also be willing to supervise their junior colleagues to whom they have delegated their project work. This is important because it is not the role of the PC or PCC to supervise these junior partners. Junior researchers need help and indeed support from their senior partners in their home countries.

Also, some partners wanted changes in timetabling early on in the project. They asked that final reports would come at the end of the overall project and not as specific projects were completed. This desire was quite reasonable, as it would take the pressure off partners to produce reports in a speedy manner.

Here, it should be noted that all of these changes were agreed at the PCC and recorded in the minutes of relevant PCC meetings. Whenever changes are made to the Technical Annex, it is the responsibility of the PC to report them in writing to the Commission. In every instance, the Commission approved these changes; however, this tended to be a protracted process. In easing this process, it is important for PCs to have a close working relationship with their Scientific Officer at the Commission. The advice and support of my Scientific Officer was invaluable. I kept her continually informed of how the project was progressing as well as the changes that we wanted.

Awareness of Diversity as the Heart of International Research

Earlier, I stated that sensitivity to diversity meant that issues such as language, race, ethnicity, nationality, gender, disability, class, age and academic

Table 1

Project management structure and basic tasks

Project tasks	Country 1	Country 2	Country 3	Country 4
Overall project coordination	**PC**			
Study A				
(a) Overall study coordinator	**PC**			
(b) Data organization	PC	Ps 4 and 5	Partner 6	Partner 7
(c) Data collection	JR1	JR 5	JR 7	Partner 7
Study B				
(a) Overall study coordinator (coordinator of common interview schedule)	**PC**			
(b) Arranging interviews	PC	Ps 4 and 5	Partner 6	Partner 7
(c) Data collection	PC	PC	PC	PC
Study C			NA	NA
(a) Overall study coordinator (coordination of common survey)	**Partner 2**			
(b) Data collection	JRs 2 and 3	Partner 5		
(c) Responsible for country study and report	Partner 2	Partner 5		
Study D				
(a) Overall study coordinator (coordination of common survey)			**Partner 6**	
(b) Data collection	JRs 2 and 3	Partner 5	JR 8	JR 9
(c) Responsible for country study and report	Partner 2	JR 6 Partner 5	JR 8	(SC)
Study Ea			NA	NA
(a) Overall study coordinator (coordination of common survey)	**Partner 2** **(JR 2+)**			
(b) Data collection	JRs 2 and 3	Partner 4		
(c) Responsible for country study and report	Partner 2	Partner 4 Partner 4		
Study Eb		NA	NA	NA
(a) Study coordinator and responsible for country study and report	**Partner 3**			
(b) Data collection	JR 4			
Study Ec		NA	NA	**Partner 7**
(a) Study coordinator				
(b) Responsible for country study and report	Partner 1			
(c) Data collection	JR 1			Partner 7
Formulation of study recommendations on a European level and production of final report		**All partners**		

PC = (Project coordinator) Partner 1, Ps = Partners, JR = Junior Researcher, SC = sub-contractor.

*Data not included in final study because they were not comparative.

+delegation to a junior researcher

NA = not applicable in specific country (i.e. was not carried out).

status are very important in guiding our research practice in international collaborative settings. PCs learn that openness to diversity is important in the successful management of a project. Ideally, one's partners should be attentive to and accept the need for cultural diversity. Regrettably, this is not always the case.

However, as most social scientists are aware, the public shaping of this key issue of diversity, particularly with regard to race, gender and class, is essential to the discourse of the nation state in European societies (Anthias and Yuval Davies 1992; Yuval Davies 1997). Nevertheless, the ways in which all of these diversities are dealt with vary from culture to culture. For example, the social statuses of researcher and professor may differ from one society to the next. These differences tend to emerge during the research process as partners position themselves for power and space on a project. Race and ethnicity or indeed disability may be issues which have high visibility in one culture but not another. A PC needs to be aware of these cultural nuances and generate a research atmosphere in which dealing with these issues can be embedded in the research process as a fundamental part of the research design.

One diversity issue which deserves close scrutiny is that of language. For example, English is the project language of research funded by the EU and this is made clear in the contract with Brussels. While many research scientists are fluent in English, the effects of English as the dominant working language must not be underestimated. For non-native English speaking academics, using a foreign language, such as English, is a complicated affair. English usage tends to be valued on the basis of whether or not: (1) one has studied, worked or lived in an English-speaking country; (2) one's home country has a strong relationship with an English-speaking nation/s; (3) one requires English in one's daily research work; and (4) one can express oneself, if and when one becomes passionate about one's work. On another level, it could be argued that speaking English in continental Europe was a skill which, until the middle of this century, was possessed mainly by the upper middle classes and aristocracy. Thus, the remnants of this sort of language transmission may signal privilege, while at the same time it is not experienced in a similar way.

When project leaders work with research partners whose mother tongue is not English, this may cause problems in a variety of areas. These problems vary and may involve misunderstandings of basic research tasks; misuse of key project concepts; difficulties with translating the project's data collection tools from English into a partner's language and vice versa; and major complications with financial reporting. Whether or not one is a native English speaker, one learns very quickly that the language of the European Union research world is "bureaucratic" and not "normal", everyday English. Predicting this sort of process, Whyte (1956) bemoaned the way the academic was seduced into the officious world of international research where the "bureaucratization of the scientist" took place. The key point is that even for the native English speaker, the bureaucratization of the English language makes it a difficult language to comprehend.

Project leaders must pay attention to this language issue and allow space for it to emerge and, furthermore, be discussed amongst partners. One strategy

Elizabeth Ettorre

I used was to say at annual project meetings that I was aware that the majority of partners were not native English speakers; I knew at times this caused them difficulties with expressing themselves and I felt strongly this should be recognized amongst the group. I also said that I appreciated that they spoke in my mother tongue, and I did not take it for granted. If this issue of the hegemony of the English language remains unrecognized, partners will tend to avoid taking responsibility for the above-mentioned problems if and when they occur.

For example, in our project, there was consistent conflict over the term "eugenics". The term is not a straightforward one in English, and it has a variety of meanings in other cultures, dependent upon a country's historical legacy. For some partners it was an uncontested concept which meant "good birth", while for others it was a politically loaded one, conjuring up images of Nazi death camps.

Given this discussion of the need for acceptance of cultural diversity, it is the duty of PCs to ensure that the research produced is neither exclusionary nor reflective primarily of the interests of dominant groups in societies that are studied. One strategy to ensure an inclusionary research framework is to discuss continually the need for "multicultural research within a multidisciplinary framework". Most, if not all, research partners will understand what multidisciplinary means, given that much contemporary work in public policy research in the social sciences is so labelled. Making the transition in one's mind from an understanding of "multidisciplinary" to an acceptance of multiculturalism may not be easy. However, generating an awareness of the need for both helps all partners to experience inclusion both in terms of their own disciplines and of their own cultures, academic lifestyle choices and levels of abilities.

EU Research Work as Group Work: the Dynamics of Research and Processual Issues

It was stated above that maintaining openness to diversity is facilitated by generating an awareness of group processes. Basically, to be an effective PC entails knowledge of how people work in groups. While I was leading Project 96, I found it very helpful to refer to texts on group work and/or feminist group work (Butler and Wintram 1991; Krzowski and Land 1988; Douglas 1976) in order to understand some of the dynamics of our particular research group. Prior to being PC, I understood the theory behind group processes. As I took on my role as PC, I began to experience these processes in practice.

There is a lack of information on *research group work*. As a result, I used a book, *Strategic Planning Workbook for Nonprofit Organizations* (Barry 1986) developed by Community Services Group in St Paul, Minnesota, as my "bible". This manual provided a detailed explanation of how to plan strategically in groups. With it, I began to form insights on how a grouping of individuals, whether they are in therapeutic, community or research groups, goes through distinct stages in becoming a group. Reflecting on these experiences, I found the work of Corey and Corey (1997) important in forming ideas on the various stages of groups. These authors discuss five group stages which include: (1) Formation stage (that is, when members are aware of the specifics of the group, may be ambivalent and involve themselves in initial power struggles); (2) Initial stage (when members begin to orient themselves to the structure and leadership of the group, test the atmosphere and search for trust); (3) Transition stage (when members experience anxiety, are concerned about what others think of them and when their defences in the form of resistance emerge); (4) Working stage (group cohesion is high and communication is open); and (5) Ending stage (when members of the group experience sadness and anxiety over the group's ending). In table 2, I have adapted these stages to research groups and developed my own ideas on how these stages affect both group members and leaders.

As the leader of our research group, I was fascinated to plot the group's transitions as they occurred during the research process. I found that being aware of these stages was essential in developing my PC role. Specifically, when I observed the group moving towards another stage, I was able not only to understand the sorts of feelings expressed by members but also to develop my leadership role in a positive way (that is, helpful to research partners). I became more confident about what was going on in the group and able to explain to myself why certain members behaved in the ways they did. In the following discussion, I provide some examples of how knowing about these stages in the group and understanding the group's processes allowed me as a project leader to become more strategic. With hindsight, I am able to identify the specific strategies I used during each stage of the group process. At that time, I used these strategies to ensure the successful completion of the research and the stable, if not smooth, running of the group. I was unaware whether or not the particular strategies would be beneficial to the group.

The Formation stage: doing diary work and charting movements of power

During the Formation stage, I started to keep a diary in which I recorded all of my thoughts and feelings on what was happening during this crucial stage. This was the stage when I observed power struggles most clearly. In my diary, I made a chart of the struggles going on between partners and/or other group members (i.e. junior researchers). Making this type of chart allowed me to map out the power dynamics of the group in an objective way and thus to understand more clearly any attempts to undermine my leadership. Although my diary was useful throughout the project, it was most useful during this first stage. At that time, I needed to consolidate my own resources as well as help group members to focus on their potential in order to prepare us for the basic tasks at hand. My diary allowed me to have an acceptable outlet for my fears and frustrations. My diary "held" these feelings and issues for me and allowed me to create charts or pictorial images of group dynamics on a daily level. It was also helpful in writing this paper.

Table 2

Stages of the research group process

Group stage	Members	PC (Leader)
Formation stage	• freely join the group • are aware of the basic research tasks and contract specifics **OR** Do not have adequate information; Are passive/ambivalent; Do not think about the implications of joining the research group	• gathers partners • explains the overall research aims and tasks of the research • submits proposal to EU **OR** Is involved in power struggle/s; Does not communicate research information adequately to the members
Initial stage	• orient themselves to the structure and leadership of the research group • test the group atmosphere • search for acceptance from other partners **OR** Are vague and non-committal; Keep worries about research to themselves	• helps partners to see ground rules and group norms • works towards group trust • clarifies basic tasks and research responsibilities for group **OR** Does not have a clear idea of the rules or norms of the project: Panics or is unclear
Transition stage	• recognize research conflicts and problems and begin to work through them • are conscious of themselves in the research process and what others think of them **OR** Form cliques; Do not express any doubts or problems about the research	• provides encouragement about the research • helps group to deal with any disagreements about the research • ensures the research gets done in the midst of any disagreements **OR** Discourages an open atmosphere; Labels some members as "problems"
Working stage	• are cohesive • communicate • research gets done **OR** Withdraw because of others' success or intensity; Become lazy and avoid challenging each other	• promotes work that leads to research completion • assists members to see links with other members' research **OR** Is too confrontational towards those who may be behind schedule; Discourages rather than encourages work
Ending stage	• are sad or anxious • make decision on future work together (i.e. project book) • offer feedback on research experience **OR** Distance themselves from the group; Complain how the research could have been better	• identifies reality that the group is ending • provides feedback on research experience and allows the same for other members • expresses gratitude to members for the successful completion of the project **OR** Does not allow feedback; Is unable to deal with saying goodbye

Note: OR indicates possible problems which can and do sometimes arise

The Initial stage: instigating the project newsletter

During the Initial stage, I noticed that while group members were getting to know each other, it was essential that information about the progression of each study be shared amongst the group in an accessible way. After the first project meeting, I instigated a project newsletter (PN) as a way of keeping lines of communication open within the group. Initially, I and my assistant produced the PN on a bimonthly basis. Group members were asked to send any information which they wanted to include in the PN to us the day before it was due to go out. As this work developed, we included not only news about the progression of studies but also important dates and events, changes of addresses of partners, abstracts of submitted papers, financial information and various policy papers. During the Transition stage of the research, I used the PN as a way of communicating to partners various problem areas. While I did not mention partners' names, I was able to describe an issue that arose with any partner and how I dealt with it. For example, an entry could read: "One partner asked me if I could change the meeting date next year from [date] to [date]. As you know this decision was made at our PCC meeting. Given that it was a group decision and that we found it difficult to find a suitable date for all partners, I said it was best that we keep to our original decision." This transmission of information was done as a way of providing information to partners in an accessible way without offending the concerned party.

As the group progressed into the Working stage, the PN was produced on a monthly basis. The PN was produced until the completion of the project. By that time we had produced 40 newsletters over a three-year period.

The Transition stage: searching for support from a consultant and group therapist

Adrian Cadbury in his "Introduction" to J. A. C. Brown's *The Social Psychology of Industry* states: "If you cannot make a reasonable stab at accounting for your own behaviour, it is hard to see how you can usefully account for the behaviour of those with whom you work" (Cadbury 1986: x). The message is that an effective leader must be self-aware, while at the same time conscious of the awareness of others in the group. For a leader to gain this sort of reflexivity within her group demands active listening, "the ability to convey the essence of what a person has communicated so that the person can see it" (Corey and Corey 1997: 69).

During the Transition stage of the project, I was aware that various conflicts had emerged concerning the methodologies as well as timetabling of two projects and as a result, some partners were unhappy. I needed more than ever to be an active listener. Because the group met at most twice a year and, more importantly, because we were working to a tight timetable, it was important that conflicts with the group be resolved quickly. I was also becoming aware that group work is not easy in two fundamental ways. First, for a group to achieve an acceptable level of compromise in order to fulfil their common task (i.e. doing the research), there will inevitably be a struggle to find that level. This is over and above the wants and needs of the group leader and members. Second, when creative work is to be done by a group, sadness or pain will necessarily precede it. With this in mind and given that I was rather inexperienced as a PC, I sought out the help of two key individuals: a mentor/consultant and a group therapist.

I approached a colleague to be my mentor because she was someone who had extensive experience in the European research world and who was a leading researcher herself. When I explained that there were certain group problems that I needed to discuss in confidence and would like her to help me look at them objectively, she agreed. From the beginning, she asked if I would use her as a consultant rather than a mentor because she wanted to maintain a level of equality with me. She felt that this type of consultation would be a learning experience for both of us. Although I offered to pay for this service, she did not want any financial remuneration. For approximately nine months, we met on a bimonthly basis. She helped me to see more clearly how conflicts came about in the research group and, more importantly, how to resolve them. We both developed our skills as "active listeners".

At this time, I had a colleague who was a group therapist. When he heard of my group's conflicts, he offered to help me to look at my particular research group through his eyes. I must admit that I found these consultations fascinating. I read parts of *Bion and Group Psychotherapy* (Pines 1985) as well as *Using Groups to Help People* (Whitaker 1985). With my colleague's help, I slowly began to see that a group might become at any one stage in its progression more important than the individuals within it. Simply, groups are able to take on a life of their own. More importantly, I learned that leading groups can open one up to what Bion (Sutherland 1985) calls the "group mentality" and that as a result one can become the target of all sorts of fears, aggression, idealization and both destructive and positive impulses. Once I became aware of these processes, I felt more confident and able to trust my own sense of leadership. I am still deeply grateful to both of my colleagues for helping me and recommend these types of consultations to any potential and current PC.

The Working stage: visiting partners' cultures while generating a sense of fairness

While I was completing Study B, I needed to visit every country to gather data. At that time, I thought it would be appropriate to make site visits to partners and to discuss the project's progression as well as my own views on the project. In this context, I want to mention that as academics, we tend to avoid any discussions of feelings or difficult interpersonal issues in our research work. If a PC is going to learn anything about herself, her management skills, professional work practices, ways of communicating to colleagues and research ethics, she must face up to her leadership style on a feelings level. This type of leadership is about cultivating a research atmosphere in which both comfortable and uncomfortable feelings can be expressed. For me, cultivating an open research atmosphere involved in practice developing a sense of fairness. While on my visits to the various partner countries, I attempted to make my leadership style clear.

I believe that when a PC knows who she is and has confidence in herself within the group, she can convey this to the research group in a powerful way. Indeed, when leaders are able to recognize and accept themselves, both their strengths and their weaknesses, this gives others in the group permission to do the same. For me this is about cultivating a sense of humility and fairness. Giving recognition where it is due or inculcating a sense of fairness in a diverse group of researchers is important, if the group is going to work as a group—to get the research done! Thus, making visible a sense of fairness helped our group become cohesive in the run-up to final stage of the project.

The Ending stage: planning "closure" during the final project meeting

Near the completion date of the project, I had been aware that all of the seven studies were in the final stages of being written up and that partners were eager to meet and to discuss their findings. Our final meeting was scheduled as a two-day weekend meeting in my university. I had planned this final project meeting carefully both in terms of venue, activities and structure because I knew that it would be the last time some of us would meet. At the beginning of the meeting, I was aware that some partners were already experiencing anxiety about the research group's ending. This became evident when a few members wanted to change the structure of the agenda and to meet in working groups. I allowed this because their request was reasonable and I knew it would allay some of their anxiety. Also, I sensed that breaking into smaller groups would also help the group in the separation process.

Basically, at this final meeting the work got done and we had a clear idea on what the final report would contain and when it would be delivered to Brussels. The meeting progressed well with only a few, minor disagreements. Before the meeting ended on the last day, I made a conscious decision to make a statement about my experience as PC. I said that I knew it was hard to say goodbye to each other and that I wanted to thank everyone for their participation in the project, although at times it was not easy. I also told them that I appreciated the diversity in the group and knew that it helped the research.

For me the most interesting decision made at this meeting was the one to do a project book. At the first meeting, I had already asked partners whether or not they were interested in my pursuing this type of project. Initially, they were not enthusiastic. However, in time many partners saw a project book as a logical extension of our work. In the context of our last meeting, I saw it as a way of continuing our collegial relationships. Indeed we are still working together and in this way the group lives on.

Sensing the Effects of Research Organizations and Topics: "DREAD" in the Midst of "Emotional Leadership"

Thus far, I have shown that project coordination on an international level is a complicated business and demands active listening, awareness of group processes and cultural diversity and at some level, conscious reflection of oneself and others. However, I would suggest that there are two further

Elizabeth Ettorre

issues which will inevitably affect research practice: the structure of partners' research organizations, and the project's research topics. These issues became visible for me after completion of Project 96 and it may be that these issues can be looked at only through hindsight and a sense of reflection.

Research organizations

Years before RAEs, Bulmer (1982: 138) pointed out that the location of research influences the type of research carried out, and he distinguished between the different types of research organizations: user organizations, university departments and special institutes. He exposed the weakness of applied research in Britain prior to the Rothschild Report of 1971 and how it was not solidly established as in other countries.

In this context, the EU demands that research be applied and achieve policy outcomes. For a PC, this means that she must be aware of the dangers of empiricism, while at the same time being sensitive to the risks of a project being driven by the needs and wants of partners' research organizations. For example, a PC must not lose sight of the fact that some partners are encouraged if not pressurized to do collaborative research by their institutions and, furthermore, that these research organizations may have few if any administrative structures in place to evaluate research quality. Furthermore, research outcomes in these organizations may be more to do with producing quantity than quality. In this sense, PCs must be sensitive to the different types of research organizations represented by their partners. One needs to search for quality while appreciating any partner's need for quantity.

Projects' research topics

The research topic of Project 96 touched upon the issue of ethics and I was continually fascinated to see how this issue of ethics intertwined with the research execution. Some partners became attentive when the word "ethics" was mentioned, while others were not at all concerned to deal with this issue. Some partners used the term "ethical" when discussing a certain research practice. At those times, my inclination was to use the word "reliable" rather than "ethical". I believed this confusion came about because partners believed at some level that they had to do "ethics" in the research process as well as study it. While this aspect of my coordination work will take another paper to explain, I wanted to flag it up in this context. PCs must be aware that the group's research topic may become visible or "acted out" in the group's research practice. The project leader needs to be conscious of this. It is not a case of allowing it to happen, it will emerge on some level. One has to be vigilant to see it and deal with it.

In conclusion, I have attempted in this paper to challenge the "senior academic = good leader" myth and to establish various benchmarks for good research management, particularly on an international level. I contended that effective research management demands sensitivity to diversity as well as an awareness of group processes in a scientific context. With hindsight, a PC becomes aware of the influences of partners' research organizations and the topic of the project. During my project coordination, I remember once saying to a colleague that to be a PC could be best described by the acronym DREAD. Somehow using this acronym took away the anxiety and fear that I had experienced in our research group, especially when I became the target of criticisms. DREAD became my catchword. Let me explain.

The D in DREAD is all about the need for a PC to *delegate* authority and to do this delegation with *responsible* partners (R). The E is all about *ensuring* that all partners have equal access to the project's resources. The A is the *allocation* of project tasks on the basis of what is agreed amongst the research partners. The final D is *disseminating* information equally amongst partners. For me, *d*elegation, *r*esponsibility, *e*nsuring access, *a*llocation of tasks and *d*issemination (DREAD) was and is an apt way to describe the PC role. For me, DREAD was a continual reminder that the first step in becoming an effective research leader or PC is overcoming one's anxiety about making mistakes as well as one's *dread* of the unknown. No one can be a perfect research coordinator, but an awareness of cultural diversity and knowledge of group dynamics helps in this task. Given that human imperfection is perhaps becoming more visible in international collaborative research, research leadership must be linked more with "reflective leadership" than ever before. This paper has been an initial, albeit incomplete, attempt to describe this type of "reflective" leadership. I hope that I have demonstrated that for this sort of "reflective" leader no joy can be compared to that of the group's common task fulfilled and the project completed successfully.

Notes

1. The Project is referred to as Project 96 in this paper.
2. In order to protect the anonymity of all research partners and researchers, I have used numbers rather than names for them as well as partner countries.
3. All EU contracts have an Annex II, the "Technical Annex" which includes the objectives, work content, project milestones and deliverables, ethics, social and economic impacts, project management structure, the partnership, exploitation plans, ongoing projects and an abstract for publication.

References

Anthias, F., and Yuval Davis, N. (1992), *Racialized Boundaries: Race, Nation, Gender, Colour and Class and the Anti-racist Struggle*, London: Routledge.

Barry, W. B. (1986), *Strategic Planning Workbook for Nonprofit Organizations*, St Paul, MN: Amherst H. Wilder Foundation.

Bulmer, M. (1982), *The Uses of Social Research: Social Investigation in Public Policy-making*, London: George Allen and Unwin.

Butler, S., and Wintram, C. (1991), *Feminist Groupwork*, London: Sage.

Cadbury, A. (1986), Introduction. In J. A. C. Brown, *The Social Psychology of Industry*, London: Penguin Books (reprinted with Introduction 1986).

Corey, M. S., and Corey, G. (1997), *Groups: Process and Practice*, Pacific Grove, CA: Brooks/Cole.

Douglas, T. (1976), *Groupwork Practice*, London: Tavistock.

Krzowski, S., and Land, P. (eds) (1988), *In Our Experience: Workshops at the Women's Therapy Centre*, London: Women's Press.

Elizabeth Ettorre

Mayor, F. (1992), The role of the social sciences in a changing Europe, *International Social Science Journal: Fifty Years of the ISSJ: A Selection of Articles*, 157: 455–9.

Pines, M. (ed.) (1985), *Bion and Group Psychotherapy*, London: Routledge and Kegan Paul.

Robertson, R., and Khondker, H. H. (1998), Discourses on globalization: preliminary considerations, *International Sociology*, 13, 1: 25–40.

Sutherland, J. D. (1985), Bion revisited: group dynamics and group psychotherapy. In M. Pines (ed.), *Bion and Group Psychotherapy*, London: Routledge and Kegan Paul, pp. 47–86.

Wallerstein, I. (1999), The heritage of sociology, the promise of social science, *Current Sociology*, 47, 1: 1–37.

Whitaker, D. S. (1985), *Using Groups to Help People*, London: Routledge.

Whyte, W. H. (1956), *The Organization Man*, New York: Doubleday Anchor Books.

Williams, M. (2000), *Science and Social Science: An Introduction*, London: Routledge.

Yuval Davis, N. (1997), *Gender and Nation*, London: Sage.

4

Integrating Participation into Research and Consultancy: A Conservation Example from Arabia

Dawn Chatty

Keywords

International research; Cultural diversity; Participation; Collaboration; Indigenous populations

Conservation in the Arabian Peninsula does not have a long historical dimension. In other parts of the world, ideas and policies of "preservation of nature" and the conservation of plant and animal species were exported in the early twentieth century with the colonial administrations of mainly France and Great Britain (Bell 1987). The Arabian Peninsula, however, was never a "colony" of a Western power. Furthermore, it had limited species of large mammals, making it unattractive for ecotourism development of wildlife reserves. Hence, conservation and ecotourism was largely irrelevant in the Arabian Peninsula for most of the twentieth century. Only as the millennium began to draw to a close did an interest in a particular form of conservation manifest itself in the region—animal reintroductions.

First in Oman, then Saudi Arabia, Jordan, Israel and Syria projects were set up in the late 1970s and 1980s to reintroduce the Arabian oryx into Arabia (Henderson 1974; Jungius 1985; Spalton 1993; Spalton *et al.* 1999; Stanley Price 1989). These projects, often couched in the contemporary developmental language of "participation" and "grassroots" support, in actuality regarded local human populations as obstacles to be overcome—either through monetary compensation or with special terms of local employment—instead of as partners in sustainable conservation and development. In Syria, the previous disregard for the Bedouin's land-use rights is now being questioned in the face of very limited local support for wildlife conservation schemes. Here, the language of participation is being used to mediate the environmental conflict between conservationists and pastoralists. After nearly two decades of "talking" participation, Syria seems to have made the leap from print into action and is making some effort to give conservation a human face. This paper explores and examines some of the efforts to put participation into research and consultancy.

Dawn Chatty

History of Development Aid in the Desert Regions of Syria

International projects and consultancies in Syria date back 50 years, as does most development aid activity in the region. Post-Second World War assistance, mainly in the shape of the Point IV Plan was grounded in an evolutionary model of development, often called modernization theory, which held the Western "developed world" up as the pinnacle of development. Achieving such a goal required a transfer of knowledge and technology and gave rise to numerous projects, consultancies and technical assistance programmes aimed at raising Syria from its "developing" status to that of a "developed" one. Beginning in the late 1950s, and after a severe drought lasting several years, international experts and consultants identified the indigenous population, the pastoral nomadic Bedouin, as the destroyers of their environment. Proof of this deterioration was asserted to be evidenced in the rapid disappearance of gazelle and oryx from the desert as well as the emergence of thorny scrub which indicated overgrazing and overstocking of domestic herds.[1] The traditional grazing territories of the Bedouin were confiscated, government research stations were set up and international agencies were called in to save this desert landscape from its indigenous nomadic inhabitants.

Although there have never been any empirical studies to support these pseudo-scientific assumptions, the Bedouin as "destroyer of the environment" has underpinned all policy and planning in the region. Such assumptions fits in perfectly with state policies of control where mobile and pastoral communities were regarded as less civilized and more difficult to manage. Programmes and projects have all been based on the exclusion of the Bedouin from their traditional lands, which have then been subjected to projects to replant, re-seed and, more recently, to reintroduce extinct species. Research stations and centres funded by international agencies have introduced exotic plants, set up plantations on confiscated grazing areas and set up re-seeding projects. After nearly twenty years of failed efforts, the government of Syria and the international agencies are beginning to look hard at their projects and at what data exist in Syria and in similar regions such as Jordan (Roeder 1996; Rae 1999; Fairhead and Leach 1996; Leybourne et al. 1993). These suggest that indigenous people do have a deep understanding of their natural resources which have not been tapped. They know how to use their resources and they exist in a "disequilibrium" (rather than an equilibrium) ecological system which often revives after rainfall or short rest periods (Behnke et al. 1993). They suggest, finally, that in many parts of Arabia it is the elite classes and not the indigenous inhabitants who are the hunters and are primarily responsible for the extinction of large mammals in the desert.

Background: the Bedouin in Arabia

The pastoral Bedouin tribes of Syria, and northern Arabia have, for decades, if not centuries, been in conflict with central governments. Often perceived as "states within states" numerous governments from the Ottoman Empire through the French Mandate period to the independent Syrian state have attempted to settle these people and turn them into easily reachable, controllable sedentary farmers. Two opposing forces have marked the last century in the desert areas: one compelling Bedouin to settle on the edges of the desert and engage in marginal agricultural production; the other forcing them to move away to seek multi-resource livelihoods and pastoral subsistence across several national borders (Abu Jaber et al. 1978; Chatty 1986, 1990, Lancaster 1981). The late 1940s and 1950s saw the culmination of several decades of sustained effort to control and break down pastoral tribal organization. Much of the tribal leadership was co-opted into the elite urban political scene, and land holdings once owned in common were increasingly registered in the names of tribal leaders of important families and converted into farms.

The 1960s was a period of strenuous government land reform, including the complete seizure of all common tribal land and the confiscation of the large tracts of land owned by tribal leaders. Following a three-year-long drought, in which over two million sheep died, the government instituted a programme to alleviate the problems caused by this ecological disaster. An internationally sponsored project was set up to revitalize the pastoral sector of the Syrian economy. Its foremost goal was to stabilize the pastoral livestock population. This proved very difficult mainly because the officials running the project did not understand Bedouin methods of animal husbandry.[2] In turn, the Bedouin had no trust in government, especially in light of the recent confiscation of grazing land, and the explosive expansion of agricultural development over nearly a third of the best rangelands of the desert (Al-Sammane 1981: 32).[3]

After a number of years of poor project results, a handful of specialists (Draz 1977) launched a campaign to convince agencies concerned with rangeland of the importance of studying the human factor. They argued that unless development programmes were in harmony with the customs and ways of life of the pastoral populations, the whole rangeland development scheme would fail. Bedouin as well as government cooperation was required in order to solve the problem. Eventually a plan was accepted to set up a programme of cooperatives whereby block applications by tribal units for control over their former traditional grazing lands were generally granted by the government. Power and responsibility within a cooperative thus remained within a tribe, giving its members a participatory role in the programme. Today perhaps two-thirds of Syria's Bedouin population belong to such cooperatives and associated schemes, although government reports (Al-Sammane 1981) suggest that number is nearly 90 per cent.

There were numerous ups and downs caused by changing legislation, and inadequate restraint on the spread of agriculture into the desert (Masri 1991). However, the current situation which allows Bedouin a participatory voice in the running of cooperatives that were set up to accommodate traditional Bedouin land use patterns, is an improvement over the uncontrolled grazing of the 1950s and the rigid government regulatory schemes of the 1960s. Flexibility and a *de facto* acceptance of traditional Bedouin systems of exploitation and marketing have resulted in a national programme of some success at both the national and local levels.

Throughout this period, however, the government had experimented with protecting and conserving flora in the desert, often integrating the structure of the cooperatives into its protectionist projects. The rationale behind these measures and pilot projects has been to attempt to rehabilitate rangelands, protect threatened plant and shrub species, and stop the incursion of thorny bush. The hope has always been that the Bedouin would appreciate the benefit of fencing and exclusion and be inspired to do the same on traditional land holdings. Unfortunately this has not happened. Instead, the Bedouin express resentment at traditional common lands being confiscated for government experiments from which they perceive that they are deriving no benefit (Chatty 1995; Roeder 1996).

Problem: Integrating Local Populations into Mainsteam Planning and Policy Making

An understanding is very gradually spreading among some experts and consultants that further disregard of the indigenous population from mainstream planning and policy making will only result in further displacement and social exclusion. For specific projects, such exclusion will result in continued failure to meet project goals. In the desert projects of Arabia such failure inevitably results in a cycle of censure and recrimination directed at the nomadic pastoralists or Bedouin for not complying with project regulations. Thus the very population that had been excluded from all stages of project development would be blamed for the failure of the project efforts (re-seeding, replanting and reintroduction of gazelle and oryx). In order to break this negative cycle some agencies have returned to the concept of "participation" and attempted to look at it in a new light. The aim is to move beyond a flippant acknowledgement of the existence of local users to a concerted effort to understand and integrate the indigenous population into project planning, design and management.

In 1992, Syria negotiated funding for a project to rehabilitate rangeland and to establish a wildlife reserve in the Palmyra desert. This project was approved, and the Food and Agriculture Organization was drawn into the operation of the project as it appeared to have a development focus (improving food security). The project proposed to address three interrelated issues: diminishing grazing land, disappearing wildlife, and increasing requirements for supplemental feeding of domestic herds. It also proposed to incorporate some of the land holdings of three cooperatives into protected ranges, to set up restrictions on access by Bedouin and their domestic herds, and to run a programme to introduce new plant species. After two years of this three-year project, it expected to have obtained a high enough "forage production . . . to enable domesticated animals and wildlife to live in harmony on the land" (FAO 1995: 7). In the third year of this project, physical boundaries were to be established and "the reserve will only be devoted to wildlife grazing" (FAO 1995: 7). In other words, at the close of the project, the Bedouin and their herds were to be excluded from an important area of rehabilitated rangeland.

The project is now in its second three-year cycle and many of its goals have not yet been achieved. Although there is a recognition that the "integration and effective collaboration of the beneficiaries to the programme" are required for sustainability, no visible effort has been made in the technical description of the project to incorporate the Bedouin in its planning, development, or implementation. The indigenous population, however, are only to be involved peripherally in the data recording process and in the discussion of results in order to "develop their awareness on environmental protection" (FAO 1995: 11). The wildlife reserve, *Taliila*, which received 8 oryx from Jordan and 16 gazelle from Saudi Arabia, will remain the home for these animals for the foreseeable future. The Bedouin have been excluded from any role in the planning and management of the reserve; even the four "local" guards at the entrances of the reserve have been recruited from the town of Palmyra.[4]

Research and Consultancy: Implementing a Working Concept of Participation

A quiet effort in the direction of true local participation, of mobilizing community resource management, of encouraging the formation of small "user" groups, and of building capacity and managing institutional change is now under way. Over the past two years workshops—initiated by the Food and Agriculture Organization—have been held at or near the site of the oryx reintroduction project. These meetings or consultations have aimed at introducing the concepts of participation into more than just the vocabulary of project personnel. Three workshops have been held bringing together government technicians, Peasant Union officials, project personnel, extension teams, and Bedouin whose traditional grazing and watering rights have been compromised by the oryx and gazelle reintroduction project and associated government plantation and re-seeding schemes. These workshops have, step by step, moved toward drawing all sides together to work towards a common goal—maintaining the wildlife reserve while at the same time permitting limited resource use by the Bedouin and associated users. The end goal is to achieve further capacity building and truly participatory resource management.

This first tentative workshop effort, initiated at the international level in an effort to put a brake on the inevitable failure which the project seemed to face, had numerous obstacles to overcome. The first hurdle, surprisingly, was in persuading the various potential participants of the importance of the effort. The local government technicians felt they knew the Bedouin well and therefore had all the information that was necessary. The international conservation consultants supported the position that the Bedouin did not know their environment and were not interested in sustainable conservation. The Bedouin, themselves, were mildly bemused at this rare effort to incorporate their ideas or opinions.

Dawn Chatty

In April 1997, just a few months after the arrival of the oryx and gazelle to *Taliila*, I was asked to set up a unique workshop which would bring together government technicians, party officials, project conservationists, wildlife experts, rural extension workers, as well as local Bedouin herders. After visiting Bedouin campsites and discussing the project—of which they claimed no prior knowledge—to ascertain their willingness to participate, I approached the official managers within government and at the project site. Along with an officer from the Food and Agriculture Organization, I organized a five-day workshop with the aim of introducing some basic concepts of participatory research: communications skills, informal interviewing, as well as mapping, ranking and scoring techniques. The participants included ten government technicians and Peasant Union members, ten Bedouin herders and five project staff members.[5] On the third day of the workshop the participants were to spend an afternoon in Bedouin tents, attempting to use their "new" participatory research skills. A number of the government technicians were unhappy with this exercise, for although they had never before been in a Bedouin tent, they were sure that Bedouin were ignorant illiterates with very little knowledge of the desert flora or fauna—despite having survived for centuries in this environment.

At the close of the workshop, in an internal evaluation, the government technicians reported that they had, surprisingly, learned much from the Bedouin. They found them to be hospitable and concerned. They exchanged information and listened to each other. The technicians learned more about the indigenous plants, water resources and behaviour of animals than they had known before. They came to understand why the Bedouin resisted some of the exotic plants that were being introduced. They also came to understand the burden which Bedouin exclusions from government controlled grazing areas placed on the community. And more important, they agreed to relax some of the rules of exclusion and to carry on meeting and undertaking participatory work (Chatty 1997a). With enthusiasm high, a follow-up second participatory workshop was recommended by the government and the international conservation managers. This was tentatively approved and scheduled for six months later.

In September 1997 the second five-day workshop was set up. The same individuals who had attended the first workshop took part in a two-day review after which the workshop was moved into a large Bedouin tent in one of the grazing reserves. Here an additional 25 Bedouin men and women attended. For the project personnel and government technicians, the workshop aims were to work further on understanding traditional knowledge and land use. The Bedouin herders had a somewhat different focus. They wished to become players, if not equal partners, in any development of ecotourism to the area. They did not wish to see the income which would be generated by tourist visits to the oryx and gazelle remain exclusively in the hands of the urban service providers. The conservation management team wished to emerge from the workshop with Bedouin promises to respect their continued exclusion from the project's re-seeded areas and plantations. In exchange they were prepared to allow limited access to a water source within *Taliila*, as well as further incentives in the form of income-generating activities for women.

This second workshop threw up a number of conflicts of interest which required ongoing consultation between the Bedouin, the sheep merchants, the farmers and project staff. However, as the consultant and facilitator, I found myself very much in sympathy with the Bedouin position (Chatty 1997b). They were prepared to make compromises, but they wanted to be a more integrated part of the project. The conservation team seemed to have become stuck looking for a "carrot" or compromise with the Bedouin which would protect the project's replanted and re-seeded areas from being grazed by Bedouin herds. The team did not seem interested in exploring a real partnership for ecotourism, or other developments. The traditional and cur- rent *de facto* land-use allocation system left the project plantations untouched in years of good rain, but vulnerable to grazing by Bedouin groups with long-established user rights to the areas in years of drought. This was not understood by the project team, nor did they wish to grasp the underlying principles of Bedouin land use. It was more convenient to use a Western model based on private property and open access (Hardin's *Tragedy of the Commons*, 1968) even though it did not fit the realities of the site. However, there remained good will on all sides and a desire to continue working together. A third workshop was provisionally set for April 1998.

My report on the outcome of the second workshop included a recom- mendation that traditional land use and resource allocation needed to be empirically studied and documented before further work could continue in developing a truly participatory conservation effort. The reason I gave this recommendation such emphasis was my hunch that once the project team understood the true manner in which traditional Bedouin practices of land and resource allocation persisted, they would be prepared to permit the Bedouin greater voice in negotiations and discussions. This report was well received in the technical units of the FAO. However, the on-site project management team was unhappy with the findings and felt that the Bedouin were being given too much attention, while the need for protection of the plants and shrubs was not.

The third workshop scheduled for April 1998 was cancelled by the project manager and instead a women's development expert was sent out to the project. During this three-month consultancy, several women's income- generating activities were set up: tailoring, embroidery and dressmaking. A number of young Bedouin girls took these courses and received diplomas in official ceremonies based in Palmyra. An evaluation at the close of this consultancy revealed that although the girls had enjoyed the classes and the new skills, they were unlikely to be able to earn an income from these act- ivities and did not find them relevant to their way of life.

By the summer of 1998, it was obvious that a serious drought had set in. Against the advice of the project managers and other international experts, the Minister of Agriculture declared all government plantations and re-seeded areas open to the Bedouin. Contrary to the open free-for-all which the pro- ject team had anticipated, Bedouin descended upon government grazing areas in an order of sorts. Only particular tribal groups appeared at certain sites, generally reflecting traditional associations of tribes with land and wells. This phenomenon indicated that the traditional tribal order continued to play a significant role in the way in which the Bedouin accessed resources. In other words, the project had failed to recognize that Bedouin traditional resource use and land allocation continued to function alongside the state's contemporary socialist forms of organization and access.

The project management, with encouragement from the FAO headquarters, decided that it would be in the interests of the project to better understand Bedouin land and resource allocation before continuing with any further efforts at developing a participatory relationship with the local community. A land-use consultancy was set up in April and May of 1999, and this was followed by the scheduling of the third participatory workshop in September 1999. Originally the third workshop had hoped to identify and invite actual tribal groups using, or having the rights of access to, lands under the control of the conservation project. But the land-use consultancy was too short-term to provide such information.[6] Instead the third workshop focused on reviewing the concepts introduced two years earlier, re-establishing trust and creating the most appropriate background for mobilizing community resource management, and managing institutional change. The working plan had entailed inviting 10 to 12 Bedouin in addition to the group of 18 which had participated in both previous workshops. However, the Minister of Agriculture wished the numbers to be doubled, in the belief that the success of the earlier sessions could be spread further afield. Hence the third workshop hosted over 50 participants on the first day, in a Bedouin guest tent put up on the edge of *Taliila*. The focus of the workshop was to encourage the understanding of "user" groups, their formation, leadership potential and the foundation for understanding how to deal with conflict resolution. At the close of the workshop, the participants and project staff put forward tentative plans to hold a fourth workshop which focused on group formation and conflict resolution (Chatty 1999). This would take place once the traditional land and resource use consultancy had been completed in the summer of 2000. The project personnel, government technicians and Bedouin herders had found a mechanism to communicate with each other and to attempt to solve their problems and difficulties. This was the "workshop" where all parties were able to participate to voice their concerns and search for ways to work together—if not as equals, then certainly without hierarchies of authority.

Conclusions

Government efforts to rehabilitate the Syrian desert rangelands in the 1960s initially failed to meet their objectives. Only when the human element was integrated into project development was there some success (Draz 1977). Thirty years on, government and international development agencies again proposed to rehabilitate parts of the desert and to establish a wildlife reserve—without any Bedouin consultation (Roeder 1996; FAO 1995). The lessons learned decades before appeared, briefly, to have been forgotten. Pastoralists cannot be separated from their animals or from their common grazing land. Furthermore, the underlying assumption of this project seemed to be again turning back to the stale assumption that it is pastoralists that are overgrazing, or overstocking, and that the solution is to reduce herd numbers and restrict their access to land in order to protect its carrying capacity. These assumption were not only wrong (see, for example, Behnke *et al.* 1993; Pimbert and Pretty 1995: 5), but simply provided a scapegoat for a problem rather than looking for sustainable solutions.

Conservation research and consultancy requires the inclusion of the indigenous, local human population. Such projects need to fully comprehend that their work is not strictly about plants and animals, but also about human users—the potential protectors and conservationists of endangered flora and fauna. In the situation of desert conservation research in Arabia, the Bedouin need to be part of the overall conservation effort. Their perceptions of the problems, the causes and the possible solutions need to be taken into account. Their needs for their own herds, their access to grazing land, water and supplemental feed need to be considered as well. For without their full participation, Bedouin will not support such projects, rendering international wildlife reintroduction efforts unsustainable in the long term.

Now, at the beginning of the new millennium, the Syrian government and its international conservation partners are finally reviewing the delicate balance which needs to be maintained between pastoralists, conservationists and the environment. The link to this balance has been sought through the application of the concept of participation. However, the term has been used for decades with very different meanings. True participation requires compromise, adjustment and a sincere effort to learn from all parties. It also requires the application of that learning to readjusting, revising, replanning and redrawing projects. Otherwise it is not participation, but simply a tool used by the stronger to control the weaker. In the case of the Syrian conservation project, the medium of true participatory research and consultancy in resource management, sustainable conservation and development is being sought. And despite some setbacks and conflicts of interest, the process appears to be ongoing.

Notes

1. Jonathan Rae suggests in his study (1999) that the emergence of thorny scrub is linked with the disappearance of camels from the desert grazing areas. Between 1930 and 1960 many camel herding tribes switched to sheep-raising in a response to market demands. Evidence strongly suggests that camels, by eating thorny scrub, play an important role in keeping this unpalatable scrub under control.
2. Bedouin animal husbandry is based on risk minimization rather than the more common western market profit motivation. See Shoup (1990: 200).
3. The Bedouin "dry-farmed" cereal crops during years of good rain, but the large-scale cultivation in this arid zone had never occurred before.
4. During a consultation visit in 1997, I engaged in a discussion of the hiring of local Bedouin for the reserve as a way of beginning to integrate them into the project. The international wildlife expert at the time rejected my suggestion, saying that "Bedouin would not work for the salaries I am offering". The sums concerned were minimal—a matter of $20 or $30 a month. The significance of local, indigenous participation for the long-term success of the project, however, seemed to have been lost on the expert.

Dawn Chatty

5. Of the project staff, only the international wildlife expert did not attend.
6. A further land-use study has been commissioned for a total of five months for February 2000 which should provide some of this information for future participatory workshops.

References

Abu Jaber, K., Gharaibeh, F., Khawasmeh, S., and Hill, A. (1978), *The Bedouin of Jordan: A People in Transition*, Amman: Royal Scientific Society.

Al-Sammane, H. (1981), *Al-Birnamij al-Suri li-Tahsin al-Mara'i wa Tarbiyat al-Aghnam* (Syrian programme for the improvement of range and sheep production), Damascus: Ministry of Agriculture and Agrarian Reform.

Behnke, R., Scoones, I., and Kerven, C. (1993), *Range Ecology at Disequilibrium*, London: Overseas Development Institute.

Bell, H. (1987), Conservation with a human face: conflict and reconciliation in African land use planning. In D. Andrew and R. Grove (eds), *Conservation in Africa: People, Policies and Practice*, Cambridge: Cambridge University Press, pp. 79–101.

Chatty, D. (1986), *From Camel to Truck*, New York: Vantage Press.

Chatty, D. (1990), The current situation of the Bedouin in Syria, Jordan and Saudi Arabia and their prospects for the future. In C. Salzman and J. Galaty (eds), *Nomads in a Changing World*, Naples: Istituto Universitario Orientale, Series Minor, pp. 123–37.

Chatty, D. (1995), *Hired Shepherds: The Marginalization and Impoverishment of Pastoralists in Jordan and Syria*, Amman: CARDNE.

Chatty, D. (1997a), *Final Report Social Participation Workshop Palmyra*, April, Rome: FAO.

Chatty, D. (1997b), *Final Report Second Social Participation Workshop Palmyra*, September, Rome: FAO.

Chatty, D. (1999), *Final Report Third Social Participation Workshop Palmyra*, September, Rome: FAO.

Draz, O. (1977), *Role of Range Management and Fodder Production*, Beirut: UNDP Regional Office for Western Asia.

Fairhead, J., and Leach, M. (1996), *Misreading the African Landscape*, Cambridge: Cambridge University Press.

FAO (1995), *Rangeland Rehabilitation and Establishment of a Wildlife Reserve in Palmyra Badia (Al-Taliba)*, Rome: FAO, Document no.GCP/SYR/003.

Hardin, G. (1968), The Tragedy of the Commons, *Science*, 162: 1243–8.

Henderson, D. (1974), The Arabian oryx: a desert tragedy, *National Parks and Conservation Magazine*, 48, 5: 15–21.

Jungius, H. (1985), The Arabian oryx: its distribution and former habitat in Oman and its reintroduction, *Journal of Oman Studies*, 8: 49–64.

Lancaster, W. (1981), *The Rwala Bedouin Today*, Cambridge: Cambridge University Press.

Leybourne, M., Jaubert, J., and Tutwiler, R. (1993), Changes in migration and feeding patterns among semi-nomadic pastoralists in northern Syria. *Pastoral Development Network Paper 34a*, London: Overseas Development Institute.

Masri, A. (1991), *The Hema Cooperatives of Syria*, Rome: FAO.

Pimbert, M., and Pretty, J. (1995), *Parks, People and Professionals: Putting Participation into Protected Area Management*, Discussion Paper 57, Geneva: United Nations Research Institute for Social Development (UNIRSD).

Rae, J. (1999), *Rangeland Management in the Syrian Steppe: Tribe and State*, DPhil thesis, Oxford University.

Roeder, H. (1996), *Socio-Economic Study of the Bishri Mountains*, Cologne: Deutsche Gesellschaft für Technische Zusammenarbeit (GTZ).

Spalton, J. (1993), A brief history of the reintroduction of the Arabian oryx (*Oryx leucoryx*) into Oman 1980–1992, *International Zoo Yearbook*, 32: 81–90.

Spalton, A., Lawrence, M., and Brend, S. (1999), Arabian oryx reintroduction in Oman: successes and setbacks, *Oryx*, 32, 2: 168–75.

Stanley Price, M. (1989), *Animal Re-introductions: the Arabian Oryx in Oman*, Cambridge Studies in Applied Ecology and Resource Management, Cambridge: Cambridge University Press.

5

Multiple Scripts and Contested Discourse in Disseminating Research Findings

Gillian Lewando Hundt

Keywords

Politics; Research; Collaboration; Dissemination

Introduction

This paper explores verbal and textual communications in international research as performances that occur within interpretive and literal (textual) frames. As performance, these events have a structure including particular settings and ground rules with participants, performers and audiences (Bauman 1978: 9). Literary criticism and reviews of plays are always diverse, with multiple often conflicting interpretations of the meaning, significance and quality of texts and performance and production. Bauman in his essays in the field of sociolinguistics in *Verbal Art as Performance* writes of how verbal art is a way of speaking:

> Fundamentally, performance as a mode of verbal communication consists in the assumption of responsibility to an audience for a display of communicative competence. This competence rests on the knowledge and ability to speak in socially appropriate ways. (1978: 11)

In research, the questions, data and findings are often understood and interpreted in different ways. These differences can sometimes be issues of differential emphasis and sometimes of contested discourse and meaning. Differences of approach or understanding often reflect the diverse positionality of stakeholders who have different structural positions, accountabilities and sensibilities. There are potential conflicts between service and research agendas, international and national priorities, scientific disciplines and ideological or political affiliations. This diversity is present in all research teams and even more acutely so in multidisciplinary research of the type funded by international agencies at this time. The way in which this diversity is explored is through an actor-oriented analysis of the research process similar to that developed by Long and Long:

we are interested in developing theoretically grounded methods of social research that allow for the elucidation of actors' interpretations and strategies and of how these interlock through processes of negotiation and accommodation. (1992: 5)

The paper reviews and discusses the multiple understandings of research questions, the process of disseminating research findings verbally and textually in two countries of an EC-funded research project. The case study is being used to highlight broader issues related to the interface between insider and outsider expertise and understandings and the influence of ideologies and politics on scientific research.

Setting

The context is a five-year EC-funded study to evaluate and improve maternal and child preventive health care to Palestinians in Gaza (Palestinian Autonomous Territories) and to Bedouin in the Negev (Israel). The institutions involved were a British University, an Israeli University and a Palestinian research centre. There were local researchers and research teams in both countries and a coordinating team in the UK led by the author. This was part of an EC Mediterranean Initiative (Avicenne) whereby the funding required the participation of a European institution with at least two partners in different Mediterranean countries. The definition of the Mediterranean included both the Mashrak (Middle East) and the Maghreb (North Africa). The research took place between 1994 and 1999. The proposal was submitted at the time of the Oslo accords in September 1993 and the research was undertaken during the ensuing "peace process" which was a time of political transition.

The structure of international collaborative research reflects international political structures and policies. Much funding comes from national and international organizations or foundations based in the northern and western hemispheres which fund work in the southern hemisphere. The funding for the specific project being used as an example here is no exception. The funds from the European Commission are distributed to countries bordering the Mediterranean in North Africa and the Middle East for research in two areas, water and health. The funding came from Directorate General I (External Affairs) and was administered by Directorate General XII (Science and Research with non-Member Countries). The rationale for this Mediterranean research programme (Avicenne Initiative) was that just as developing trade between the European countries was seen as a means to prevent future wars within Europe, so too would research on water and health (two essential resources) link countries around the Mediterranean in North Africa and the Middle East. The structure is colonial in terms of the flow of money and also by the requirement that a European research institution be involved. More often than not the European researchers in their base institution take on the lead, or in Eurospeak "coordinating", role since they have a well-resourced infrastructure (Lewando Hundt 1996). Within this structure, there are issues of external and internal expertise and multiple understandings of the nature of research and its findings.

In this project, there were two researchers based at a UK university which had the coordinating role and two research teams in the Middle East. The Palestinian team was based at the Gaza Health Services Research Centre, Gaza City, which at that time was within the Ministry of Health of the Palestinian Authority. The three researchers leading the team had training in epidemiology and public health but also had service responsibilities, two of them within the Ministry of Health and one of them within the United Nations Relief and Works Agency (UNRWA). The Israeli team was located in the Faculty of Health Sciences (a community-oriented medical school) at Ben Gurion University of the Negev, Beersheba. Some of the researchers leading the team had service responsibilities. One was working within the Ministry of Health and there were two family doctors involved, one in the first year and the other in the subsequent four years of the project. They all had part-time university appointments within the medical school.

From the outset of international research collaborations, it is common that there are differences between the various players as to the research questions being studied. These can be accommodated and seen as part of the richness of the multidisciplinary approach and the interface between research, policy and practice but these different interests influence understandings, behaviour and reactions. Reflecting retrospectively on the reasons for the differences can cast light on behaviour which at the time seemed "irrational" or difficult to understand.

In this project, the research design, data collection, analysis and dissemination were influenced by differences in and between disciplinary perspectives, namely anthropology and epidemiology, local, national and international policy agendas, service and research priorities. These differences were played out in the use of language both orally and textually.

Multiple Research Questions

Some differences in multidisciplinary research can be attributed to the formal research training of the participants. The local researchers were almost all epidemiologists by training and the UK team members were anthropologists. There was a consensus that the project was combining anthropology and epidemiology but there was a tension between which was the primary discipline and how they could be combined. Or, to put it another way, which discipline shaped the research questions. Some of the local researchers on both teams had policy and service responsibilities within their respective Ministries of Health that the external social scientists did not. They often had different agendas and priorities owing to their professional positions. The differences in approach were therefore due to external versus internal concerns, as well as interdisciplinary differences.

Understandably, those having responsibility for providing health care and with a background in epidemiology were concerned with the extent of coverage, with understanding why some women were non-attenders, and with taking measures to increase the coverage of care. So the local investigators with responsibilities for policy development and service provision emphasized the behaviour and knowledge of users: Why don't mothers attend prenatal care? How informed are they? How can we encourage them to attend the clinics and benefit from the care we offer?

The social scientists were not local but members of the UK team, with the exception of one who was only involved in the first year of the study, and they had no local service responsibility. They were more concerned with eliciting and understanding the views and experiences of users of the services and of health personnel in order to see what they wanted improved and developed in the existing provision. The external social scientists were keener to focus on the views and experience of both users and health personnel: What are the views and experiences of attenders and non-attenders? What is the nature of the care they receive? What are the clinic conditions like for the staff in these clinics? What are their views? If women do not attend the clinics, where do they go? What do they gain by attending? How would they like the provision improved?

These differences in emphasis were not incompatible and indeed were part of the group learning and understanding that developed concerning the complexity of provision. The service providers were used to measuring service provision and efficiency in numbers of patients, vaccines, clinic visits. They were interested in identifying what worked and where there were gaps in provision. The differences in approach and discipline were accommodated by the division of the data collection and analysis. The epidemiologists took prime responsibility for the questionnaires and the anthropologists took prime responsibility for the group and in-depth interviews. In addition, since the anthropologists were more focused on capturing experience and events they would identify issues that were "interesting" that seemed of marginal significance to their local colleagues.

In general in research using the deductive positivist paradigm, the research design is prepared to test a hypothesis and answer a question. In inductive interpretative research, there is more room for developing new directions and being led by the data. The studies managed to do both but this was sometimes disconcerting for those more used to more purely deductive approach. However, the lead investigators in both teams by the end of the study had developed an appreciation of a multidisciplinary approach.

One of the Israeli epidemiologists interviewed in 1999 felt that she had learnt how to combine qualitative data with epidemiological data. Previously she had perceived qualitative research as a different and separate kind from quantitative research, each with its own merits. This study was the first time she saw how much could be gained by combining them. She is now convinced that one really needs the two for a fuller picture when investigating a research question. Initially she had thought that with qualitative data there was no gold standard to assess its validity as a means of validation and that the two types of methods were measuring different things. But she was now clear that you can measure the same thing with different methods (Interview notes: August 1999). Triangulation—using several different methods to measure or ascertain data on the same topic—is a recognized way of increasing

---

Box 1

Addresses in Gaza

In the Gaza study, there was a practical field problem in finding the mothers to inter-view in the three neighbourhoods. They were a random sample selected from the registration of births held on the Management Information System. The interviewers found that all the addresses were incomplete but that the actual birth information was very accurate. The team developed alternative strategies for finding mothers based on working through clinic staff in each locality who knew the mothers by name (again incomplete addresses on health records) and in particular with well-known figures in these neighbourhoods: the driver who took them out interviewing and the staff nurse of the clinic in Jebalia. This could have been left as a problem in data collection which was resolved but one of the anthropologists saw this as interesting in itself. The accuracy of other information about births—date, sex, place, parents—contrasted starkly with the lack of address. Initially the statisticians and epidemiologists and providers were mystified by her insistence that this was interesting. She saw it as part of the social construction of statistics and persuaded the team to review how information came on to the birth register from the hospital via the clerk to the ministries. Fieldwork identified problems with birthweight in addition to addresses and led to interventions to improve the accuracy of this data. The quantitative members of the team realized that the qualitative approach was able to validate the reliability and validity of the data on the Management Information system (Lewando Hundt et al. 1999).

---

the reliability and validity of qualitative data. It can involve different types of qualitative data or quantitative data or a mixture of the two.

Issues of concern internationally were also of little concern to the local researchers, who were more interested in improving their coverage of the population in the region and nationally. For example, at the time of the research there was some international debate concerning what is the extent of care for women in terms of their general reproductive health within Maternal and Child Health (MCH) clinics. Are the clinics exclusively focusing on women when they are pregnant, and on babies needing immunization, without considering gynaecological morbidity or family spacing needs? The argument had been presented forcefully in the *Lancet* in 1985 in a paper by Rosenfield and Maine entitled "Maternal Mortality: a neglected tragedy: Where is the M in MCH?" The international meetings in Cairo and Beijing that occurred during the research focused on women's rights to choice in reproduction. In addition, there was at that time, in 1994, debate concerning the optimum number of visits needed for antenatal care with some voicing the view that fewer clinic visits during pregnancy would be sufficient in poorly resourced countries.

The EC scientific officer raised these issues on a site visit with the Israeli investigators in early 1994, prior to confirmation of funding, but there was a complete local lack of interest, knowledge or understanding of the ongoing international debate. The concern of the researcher, who was also a service provider, was to encourage non-attending women to attend prenatal care when pregnant and for those who register in the second or third trimester during pregnancy to register earlier so that adequate screening and surveillance could be offered within the preferred number of 6–8 visits during a pregnancy.

Disseminating Findings: International and Local Agendas

The dissemination of findings locally and internationally raised issues of multiple scripts and contested discourse which were specific to this setting but are also pertinent to many research settings. In both Gaza and the Negev, the local investigators would have been content to plan the interventions through reflection on the findings, without further consultation with health personnel or community representatives. This would have been in keeping with the accepted way of doing things in their settings, which is fairly hierarchical. Policy and operational decisions are made in both settings within the Ministry and carried out by health personnel without mechanisms for consultation at the clinic or community level.

The push for local dissemination was something which European funding agencies (DFID, EC, ESRC) emphasize. The ESRC has sections on its research forms which require the applicants to elaborate on how the research will be disseminated and how it will be of use. There is also an information booklet on Dissemination (ESRC 1999). In this research project, dissemination was part of the research design and was felt by the European researchers to be an essential stage in the development of local interventions. One of the main components of the research design had been that it was eliciting the views of local users and local health personnel about service provision prior to developing interventions. This concern with consultation and dissemination was an important part of applied anthropological practice and part of the current research ethos in Europe. Carrying this out within two Ministries of Health in the Middle East where dissemination and consultation with users and staff were not a priority was not straightforward for there were different audiences to address and different types of presentation and performances to be drawn up. The commitment to this part of the research was part of an external agenda.

A first step in this process was to summarize the main findings in an accessible format in the local languages for dissemination and discussion. The Palestinian team was keen to have this report for wide circulation in English and Arabic. The English text was prepared in London and then translated into Arabic by a Palestinian member of the London team with suggestions from a member of the Gaza team who visited London for this purpose. The report was then bound in a single volume using different colour paper for the English and Arabic.

There was some reluctance from a senior member of the Israeli team to have the report available in Arabic and Hebrew. Limited circulation amongst English speakers only was preferred, which was a strategy which would have excluded most of the nurses and Bedouin from perusal and discussion of the findings and their implications. The first draft of the report was prepared in English by the Israeli team and then was shortened, edited and translated into Arabic in London. Parts of it were then translated into Hebrew by a member of the Israeli team. The final version had the three languages bound in a single volume with different coloured paper for each language.

There were local sensitivities concerning not only the availability of the findings in local languages but also how to present the data in terms of fora and use of words. These sensitivities centred around different understandings of the use of language and terminology, due to political sensitivities as well as different approaches to the data.

One of the first indications of these hidden minefields and multiple understandings was a team meeting held in Gaza when data collection had just been completed. The meeting was informal and involved members of the team and other policy makers and health professionals who had been marginally involved with the study. The audience consisted of members of the research team, the research centre and a few health service managers. In all, approximately 20 people attended. The study findings were presented with the quantitative data on the study sample taking the first 45 minutes. The epidemiologist presented some tables showing the demographic characteristics of the sample in the three neighbourhoods followed by some cross-tabulations showing the utilization of antenatal care (patchy), immunization (near total coverage) and postnatal care (practically non-existent) amidst lively discussion. Some examples of qualitative data on particular topics took up the next 40 minutes, presented by the London team. As a taster to show what qualitative data were like, some quotes from a large number of focus group interviews on drug shortages and waiting times at the clinic were presented. They expressed the views of women who did not like waiting. The issue concerned how some people waiting in line at the clinic used patronage and influence to jump the queue for the nurse or doctor. Some quotes from both staff and patients were presented which showed that people used influence to get care more quickly. Although everyone understood this and would use influence if they could, both users and staff felt this practice disrupted clinic routine.

This presentation was made with the intention of stimulating a discussion about the need to address waiting times in the clinics and to illustrate the fact that the practice of exercising influence to jump the queue was disliked by both patients and health personnel. The effect of the overheads was unexpected for they provoked an explosive and agitated discussion along the lines shown in box 2.

On reflection, the first meeting was planned as a straightforward information-giving exercise. There was little preparation and practitioners of each discipline presented their own type of data. No thought was given to the wider sociopolitical context. The result was that both the methods and the findings were challenged. The second meeting was planned to get results and be taken seriously so that evidence-based interventions could be developed. The report interfaced the different types of data around selected themes relating to possible interventions, the Ministry of Health endorsed it and the findings were framed within an all-day event in a pleasant setting with a substantial meal.

In Gaza, a meeting was held at a local hotel for about 60 participants. The invitations were sent out with the document. The Minister of Health opened

---

Box 2

Initial presentation of findings and the discussion

Quotes shown on 2 overhead slides
Views of health personnel
"Wasta [using influence or connections] is how I was employed and how many were employed recently. Wasta also plays a role in getting health care quickly."
"Wasta is a big problem that has exploded in Gaza. It's a disaster. It also destroys the work system in the clinic."
"Wasta is called Vitamin W and it is everywhere in the country."
"I am ready to implement the rules once they are standardized throughout the system."
"Wasta is widely spread: it's a disastrous, destructive attitude which should be faced and eradicated."
Views of female users
"Wasta in the clinic is wrong and must be stopped. If I have an opportunity to use wasta I will use it like other people do. I know this is wrong but what can I do when everybody uses it."
"I get very disturbed by wasta but if I know someone in the clinic who tells me to 'come in, go straight in' I certainly won't lose this chance because my child is ill and I have left my other children at home alone. What might limit or eliminate wasta is organizing work in the clinic with certain regulations. People will accept this if it is followed and supported by the doctors and staff."
"I feel upset by wasta; I hate it. Everybody goes to the clinic for the same reasons. It drives me crazy when I see people using it because I believe it is wrong and that my child is not better than other children."

Resulting discussion amongst managers and researchers
Participant
"This is political talk, incited by foreigners using unscientific methods. No one talks like this. This is dangerous talk."
Senior members of the research team
"We must accept reality, all of it even if we do not like it."
"The research was carried out by local interviewers using focus groups which is an established method of enquiry. This is our study and the London team would not publish anything we did not agree with."
"You are in denial: of course people talk like this."
"These quotes are discussing the use of influence in the clinic, queue jumping in the clinic. We are not talking about corruption in the Authority. We are talking about favours which disrupt clinic routine."
Participant
"Favours, acquaintanceship, well that is part of our culture and of many cultures. It is even part of English culture in London."

---

the meeting and endorsed the importance of evidence-based health reform. Each section of the findings was presented based around topics using a combination of quantitative and qualitative data, and the possible options for intervention were discussed. There was a lively morning followed by a convivial lunch. The next day a smaller group of policy makers met all day to firm up action plans in different targeted areas. In addition, there were smaller workshops, held in clinics where interventions would be based, to share the research findings and approach to interventions with the staff who had been interviewees during the data collection. This led to the identification of a number of possible interventions and the formation of an intervention committee that met regularly during the next year and a half to monitor the progress of model interventions.

Similarly in the Negev the first team retreat to discuss initial findings was difficult—some of the findings were contested and certain terms were considered contentious. The meeting was with the research team, with in addition the supervisor of the nurses in the clinics serving the Bedouin and the head nurse of the Ministry of Health in the region.

There was some nervousness expressed by an investigator with a dual role as researcher and service provider concerning the views of the Bedouin men and women which expressed their dissatisfaction with aspects of care—the lack of staff and clinics, which was generating problems of access, and in particular their requests to be treated with more respect and politeness. These findings at the request of this investigator were not presented at this meeting much to the distress of some of the more junior members of the research team and of the UK team. In addition at lunchtime the head nurse commented that the discussion was too political and we were advised to substitute the word "social" for "political".

In appeasing the sensitivities of gatekeepers, Bedouin women's voices were muted as were more junior Arab members of the research team and the integrity of the research findings was felt by some to be at risk. There was some local reluctance to translate the report on interim findings from English into Hebrew and Arabic but this was not the consensus of the research team. This was overcome by doing the Arabic translation in London and one of the investigators based at the University did the Hebrew translation, although this was less extensive than the English or the Arabic. Meetings for dissemination and the planning of interventions were held, but with two separate groups—the nurses in the MoH clinics providing MCH care to the Bedouin and the headmasters and officials in the Ministry of Education in the Bedouin schools. The nurses did not receive copies of the findings in a bound document but the teachers did. Both meetings were low-profile events geared to a targeted limited audience of practitioners and middle managers rather than policy makers or activists.

Thus we learnt painfully that dissemination was not just a matter of the data transmission. The presentation in terms of place, messenger and design was as important as the data. We had to consider the sensitivities of the health system and society we were working within, in order to disseminate effectively. Sometimes local sensitivities prevented or limited the dissemination of information. This was something that none of the team had consciously considered. The culture, ethos and structure of the health service, the wider society and the researchers was as relevant as the research subjects, methods and data. Colleagues who were both researchers and civil servants were in a difficult situation of negotiating sometimes conflicting agendas—those of service and research and the internal versus the external.

Contested Discourse and Hidden Transcripts

When we began to disseminate the findings in academic papers a new set of problems needed to be negotiated in terms of the language and terminology to be used in describing the setting and groups undergoing political transition with a history of conflict. History reflects the ideology and politics of the time and we found that this was a contested area when writing reports and papers. Also in the Palestinian setting, criticism of the political situation was not permitted and would make the local researchers vulnerable to unpleasantness. Language was loaded with meanings which were part of the particular history and current politics of the area. What was acceptable had to be negotiated in each setting and each paper, depending on the audience and the views of the authors, team members or workshop participants.

In Gaza, the ancient history of the port of Gaza was not contentious but any reference to the organization of health care under the Israeli Civil Administration was considered too sensitive and political. A stated preference by the population for Israeli drugs rather than Palestinian products was obscured by calling the Israeli drugs "foreign". The context of care had to be ahistorical. Recent history was too difficult to write about other than as a general reference to the Intifada. All articles were proofread by the UK and Gaza investigators and the final text was always a composite version that satisfied everyone's sensitivities. One device used several times was to quote other writers on the recent past so that it was covered but was not an expression of authors' opinions. An example of this from the Background section of a published paper is as follows:

> Indeed the Palestinian National Authority links falling income to the fact that frequent and prolonged border closures during 1995–6 resulted in increased unemployment. "The majority of the Palestinian labor force still depends for a livelihood on the daily earning of a low wage in Israel due to the lack of enough jobs in Palestine. Recently, there has been a sharp downturn in wage income from Israel which occurs from time to time as a result of frequent, alleged, security closures of the borders between Gaza, West Bank and Israel" (Palestine National Authority 1997: 10). (Beckerleg *et al.* 1999: 1491)

Even placenames were contentious. Although we referred to Palestine as the place we were working in, in papers this became Palestinian Autonomous Territories as an official address. Hebrew and Arabic refer to the same places differently. In Hebrew one said the "Negev" and "Beersheva", in Arabic the "Negeb" and "Beersheba". The difference was not only linguistic but also signified a political affiliation. The way language was used and written was part of expressing postcolonial nationhood in both settings (Thiong'o 1995).

In the Negev there was a central problem about what to call the Bedouin when writing about them. There were contested discourses within the team that reflected the diversity within Israeli society and outside the country. Were the Negev Bedouin to be called simply Bedouin, Bedouin Arabs, Palestinian

Israelis, Israeli Arabs, Israeli citizens. There was a lack of agreement within the teams and amongst the Bedouin. The terms were loaded with the way in which they had been used in the past within policies and politics. It was hard to navigate through this at a time of transition.

Palestinians were people who lived in Palestine prior to the establishment of the state of Israel. Subsequently Palestinians living outside Palestine were called Palestinians and those remaining in Israel were called Israeli Arabs in local Israeli political discourse. The Bedouin were referred to by government administrators and researchers as the Negev Bedouin, a subgroup of Israeli Arabs. They called themselves *alarab* (the Arabs) and only called themselves *badoo* (Bedouin) when comparing themselves to other groups such as *fellaheen* (peasants). They also saw themselves as Palestinians but only expressed this in public on rare occasions up to the mid-1970s. The difference between the Bedouin and other Arabs in Israel was emphasized by administrators who saw the Bedouin as less political. The educational infrastructure was weaker and people were more dispersed.[1]

There is some variety in the written and oral discourse. Researchers on the whole write of Negev Bedouin, Negev Bedouin Arabs (Marx 1967). Some increasingly write about Palestinian Israelis (Espanioly 1994; Rabinowitz 1998). Government administrators talk of the Bedouin and in the past have put an emphasis on how different the Bedouin are from other Arabs in Israel—less politicized, less educated. Policies have been different for this group. They may serve voluntarily in the army. State policy could be seen as a policy of divide and rule on the grounds that within the Palestinian Arab minority in Israel only the Druze and Bedouin groups are allowed to serve in the Israeli Defence Forces (IDF). In addition there are local administrative policies in allocation of land and resources which emphasize tribal affiliations and thus perpetuate a lack of unity amongst the Negev Bedouin.

The Palestinian team in Gaza perceived and spoke of the Bedouin as our "sisters and brothers", Palestinians who had remained in 1948 and who were now Israeli citizens. The Jewish and Arab members of the Israeli research team had differences too in the terms they used in daily language depending on whom they were speaking to. Some Jewish members of the Israeli team referred to the Occupied Territories even when they were Autonomous Territories in a workshop in 1997, four years after the Oslo agreement. Moving from old-speak to new-speak is not simple or automatic and reflects personal understandings of national and international politics.

So there was a lack of agreement amongst the research teams about how to describe the history of this group, and how to refer to them in papers and reports. All texts were read by members of the team and a compromise accepted for joint papers. The specific terms of this are not the issue. What is important is how ideology and politics affect even the terms in which you refer to or name a group. This is not a neutral issue and it changes over time. These changes at a time of transition are particularly important.

An example of the type of comments when writing a joint paper and trying to negotiate and communicate the diversity and commonality is shown in box 3. The initial first draft from London had a cryptic heading in the setting section and then went on to give a general background.

Box 3

Drafts of Setting section of a joint paper
Negev Bedouin—Palestinian Israelis

The Negev, two-thirds of the land area of Israel, contains 7 per cent of the population of Israel. The Bedouin comprise 23 per cent of the population of the Negev. At the time of data collection in 1995 the population of the Negev Bedouin Arabs was officially reported to be 88,300 (Statistical Abstract of Israel 1996) (although this is considered by many to be an underestimate and that the true figure in 1995 was 90,000–95,00). Prior to the establishment of the state of Israel in 1948, there were estimated to be 50–70,000 Bedouin Arabs in the Negev. During the war of 1948, many Bedouin left the area for Egypt and Jordan and became Palestinian refugees. Approximately 11,000 remained and became Israeli citizens (Marx 1967). Bedouin Arabs have been in the Negev since the sixth century, having migrated from the Arabian peninsula. Until recently Negev Bedouin Arabs were a semi-nomadic population living from herding sheep, goats and camels and growing winter barley and wheat. Many Bedouin Arabs in Jordan, Syria, and Egypt are being settled in agricultural villages, whereas in Israel, they are being settled in towns. *It has become increasingly difficult to live a semi-nomadic life, as much of the Negev is given over to Jewish agricultural settlements, industrial and urban developments and closed military areas.*

The response from one of the Israeli co-investigators was as follows:

"I think the terms used to describe the Bedouins are very confusing. I believe that using the terms Palestinians makes one think that they are not Israeli citizens. How about: the Negev Bedouin are Muslim Arab Israeli citizens? If you think Palestinian is essential, I think some extra explanation is needed. I would say agricultural, industrial and urban development (the word 'settlement' makes them sound like Jewish settlements on the West Bank)."

The next draft had the subheading removed, modified the reference to agricultural settlements and added in two sentences at the end of the paragraph which were acceptable to all the authors.
Setting
... It has become increasingly difficult to live a semi-nomadic life, as much of the Negev is given over to agriculture, industry, towns and areas for military manoeuvres including three airports. *The Negev Bedouin are Israeli citizens and form part of the minority Palestinian Arab population of Israel today. They are Sunni Muslims.*

This version was acceptable to both the authors and the reviewers and is currently in press. (emphasis added)

Discussion

The performance of international multidisciplinary research is situated in a number of "battlefields of knowledge" (Long and Long 1992). It seems mistaken to consider only disciplinary differences. The social and political context of the research funding, implementation and dissemination is critical. There is a need for sensitive reflection on how ideologies, politics and pragmatic survival strategies impinge on scientific questions and the use of language in text and oral performance. It seems that external researchers working in a local setting as a guest or visitor and colleague need to consider constantly "the importance of treating knowing as a practical, situated activity, constituted by a past, but changing, history of practices" (Hobart 1993: 17).

Cohen, in his fieldwork in the Outer Hebrides, comments: "Modes of knowledge are inextricable from modes of identity. 'Facts', 'knowledge' are not treated on their inherent merits even if it was possible to establish what these might be. They are assimilated to and evaluated in the light of the social position of the perceiver" (Cohen 1993: 39).

Social scientists tend to remember this when working with informants or subjects rather than bearing this in mind when working with other researchers and policy makers. There may be a tendency to assume that lack of agreement on research design or interventions is about intellectual or interdisciplinary differences rather than being connected to local political and professional constraints. The complexity of our own social worlds is often baffling to ourselves. Negotiating within the constraints of others' social and political worlds is a hazardous enterprise.

It is clear that local researchers with service or policy responsibilities are often caught between conflicting internal and external agendas. As Hobart writes:

> There is an unbridgeable, but largely unappreciated gap between the neat rationality of development agencies' representations which imagine the world as ordered or manageable and the actualities of situated social practices, an incommensurability tidied away in sociological jargon as "unintended consequences". The result is that the overlap of developers and local discourses does not lead to improved communication, but to strain on those locals who are involved in both, and to techniques of evasion, silence and dissimulation. (Hobart 1993: 16)

In these two settings, the local researchers had constraints owing to local political issues and ideologies and there were different positions and opinions within each team that reflected the diversity within each country. I would argue that the analysis and examination of these contested discourses and multiple scripts is an essential aspect of understanding the performance of research in both its oral and written forms. By articulating, negotiating and valuing these differences, the knowledge is situated within both international and local contexts.

The practice of research can only be improved if the politics of research are problematized and considered as part of the research setting. The approach of reflexive anthropology with its consideration of multiple scripts and contested discourses in text and language can only enhance the performance and enterprise of research in a complex, socially constructed world, particularly in international collaborative research, when external and internal expertise and agendas jostle against and inform each other. It is suggested that an explicit recognition and exploration of the diversity and multiple voices and views within research teams as part of research planning and implementation would facilitate and enhance the research process and findings.

Acknowledgements

This research was supported by DGXII of the European Commission, Avicenne 31. I would like to thank the members of the research teams who were part of this project between 1994 and 1999 and for their willingness to reflect on the research process subsequently. The reflective research on the politics of research was supported by a Research Fellowship from the Leverhulme Trust during 1999–2000.

Note

1. There are several reasons for this. Before high schools in the Negev were well established Bedouin boys would go to the Triangle in the middle of the country for their secondary education before returning to the Negev for further study or work. The occupation of the West Bank and Gaza enabled people to re-establish contact with their kin and to see how their lives had developed since 1948. This ended twenty years of isolation from other Arabs and all Palestinians outside Israel. The 1973 war restored some pride also concerning Arab military capabilities and this was followed by the revival of Islam which manifested itself amongst the Bedouin by the establishment of mosques and the growth of the Islamic party. The war in Lebanon was seen as clearly against the Palestinians and resulted in identification with the victims and not the aggressor. The Intifada continued this and the establishment of the Palestinian Authority has given added weight to their shared ethnicity and nationhood with other Palestinians whilst simultaneously being Israeli citizens and Bedouin. Although administrators, researchers and the media may persist in emphasizing the cultural difference of the Bedouin, there has developed a much greater awareness, identification and activism with other Palestinians in both the Palestinian Autonomous Territories and within Israel.

References

Bauman, R. (1978), *Verbal Art as Performance*, Rowley, MA: Newbury House.

Beckerleg, S., Lewando-Hundt, G., Abed, Y., Eddama, M., El Alem, A., and Shawaa, R. (1999), Purchasing a quick fix from private pharmacies in the Gaza Strip, *Social Science and Medicine*, 49, 11: 1489–1500.

Cohen, A. P. (1993), Segmentary knowledge: a Whalsay sketch. In M. Hobart (ed.), *An Anthropological Critique of Development: The Growth of Ignorance*, London: Routledge, pp. 31–43.

ESRC (1999), *Pressing Home your Findings: Media Guidelines for ESRC Researchers*, Swindon: ESRC.

Espanioly, N. (1994), Palestinian women in Israel: identity in light of the Occupation. In T. Mayer (ed.), *Women and the Israeli Occupation*, London: Routledge, pp. 106–20.

Fardon, R. (1990), *Localizing Strategies, Regional Traditions of Ethnographic Writing*, Edinburgh: Scottish Academic Press and Smithsonian Institution Press.

Hobart, M. (1993), Introduction: the growth of ignorance? In M. Hobart (ed.), *An Anthropological Critique of Development: The Growth of Ignorance*, London: Routledge, pp. 1–31.

Gillian Lewando Hundt

Lewando-Hundt, G. (1996), Rhetoric and reality in European cooperation with third Countries, *Social Policy and Administration*, 30, 4: 368–81.

Lewando-Hundt, G., Abed, Y., Skeik, M., El Alem, A., and Beckerleg, S. (1999), Addressing birth in Gaza: improving vital registration using qualitative methods, *Social Science and Medicine*, 48, 6: 833–43.

Long, N., and Long, A. (1992), *Battlefields of Knowledge: The Interlocking of Theory and Practice in Social Research and Development*, London and New York: Routledge.

Marx, E. (1967), *Bedouins of the Negev*, Manchester: Manchester University Press.

Rabinowitz, D. (1998), *Anthropology and the Palestinians*, Israel: Institute for Israeli Arab Studies (Hebrew).

Rosenfield, A., and Maine, D. (1985), Maternal mortality; a neglected tragedy. Where is the M in MCH?, *Lancet*, ii: 83.

Palestinian National Authority (1997), *The Status of Health Statistics in Palestine: Annual Report 1996*, Palestine: Health Research and Planning Directorate, Statistics and Information Department, Ministry of Health.

Thiong'o, Ngugi wa (1995), The language of African Literature. In B. Ashcroft, G. Griffiths, and H. Tiffin (eds), *The Post-colonial Studies Reader*, London: Routledge, pp. 285–90.

Unpublished reports

Lewando-Hundt et al. (1998), *Evaluation of Maternal and Child Health Care amongst the Negev Bedouin, Interim Findings*, London School of Hygiene and Tropical Medicine/ Ben Gurion University of the Negev.

Lewando-Hundt et al. (1997), *Evaluation of Maternal and Child Health Care in Gaza, Summary Findings*, London School of Hygiene and Tropical Medicine/Gaza Health Services Research Centre.

6

Researching a Contemporary Archive

Catherine Jones Finer

Keywords

International voluntary aid; Borrelli; Street children; Naples

Introduction

Being offered free access to a private collection of documents relating to the lifetime's work of a charismatic social reformer, with a view to writing a book about it and him, is the sort of proposition some academics can find it hard to resist. Certainly it was true of this author, when she was invited to work through the extensive records of the one-time famous *Casa dello Scugnizzo* of Naples, by its founder Mario Borrelli, on the eve of his own retirement. The prospect seemed one of a ready-made research project based, moreover, in an attractive location. Its attractions were yet further enhanced by the award of a small grant from the Nuffield Foundation [£2,580 awarded in November 1996[1]] towards the costs of the author's research activity in Naples, to be spread over three university vacations in the course of 1997.

Yet there is some truth in the saying "the one thing worse than *not* getting what you want can be *getting* what you want". In this case the offer was of unlimited (and by the same token undirected) access to the contents of a huge assortment of papers, of varying focus, quality and import; whose own immediate future was uncertain and whose location was continually subject to change, as the new management of the *Casa dello Scugnizzo* premises (now functioning as the *Materdei* Community Centre) struggled to make the best use of the space it had inherited, and as Mario Borrelli took what steps he could to protect his records.

The purpose of the present paper is to highlight some of the difficulties and dilemmas arising from this particular experience, as a caution to others who might find themselves similarly placed, when researching contemporary history.

The Open-ended Invitation

Few invitations turn out to be genuinely without strings, whatever the inviter's best intention. The very offer of such an invitation implies a presumption of shared values and interests. In this case there was indeed an unwritten agreement between Mario Borrelli and the author, that the purpose of the research would be to compile a dispassionate, substantial account of his work in the field of social action and reform, such as could be taken seriously by an international audience of social science academics and practitioners. Manifestly this was not to be (yet another) exercise in hagiography (see Appendix). Neither was it to be an exercise in political or social propaganda.

At best this was an informal understanding, yet there were reasonable grounds for expecting it to work in practice. Mario Borrelli had enjoyed a long fund-raising and campaigning relationship with Britain, and had himself studied successfully for a Masters degree in Social Administration at the London School of Economics (1968–70). The author had also studied Social Administration at the LSE. Indeed it was a summer fieldwork assignment from the LSE which had first introduced her to the *Casa dello Scugnizzo* in 1964—a harbinger, as it turned out, of her subsequent interest in comparative and international social policy. So this was a prospective "partnership" with much to recommend it: a combination of practitioner expertise and academic experience based on at least an element of common grounding in applied social science. Nevertheless, given the scale of the project in prospect, there was still ample scope for differences of priority and preference to make themselves felt; as indeed they did.

Mario Borrelli wished to be taken seriously as a multi-faceted social reformer. For him, therefore, it was the *entirety* of his work, both in Naples and on the European stage, which was, ideally, to be under review. Notably this included his involvement with the "spontaneous groups" (mostly fresh-recruited, concerned university students) of the 1960s campaigns to clear the shanty towns in Naples. Equally it included his involvement, from the 1970s especially, in international debates and conferences on the themes of "peace education, research and action" under the auspices of the ostensibly academic International Peace Research Association (IPRA).[2] Additionally, it involved his work for the Council of Europe's Inquiry into Street Children, by which he had been commissioned to document the incidence and plight of the same ("children *of* the street, not merely *in* the street") in Spain and Portugal, as well as Italy (Council of Europe 1994).

Borrelli's expectation amounted to a tall order, and one rather removed from what the researcher herself had had in mind. *Her* prime interest lay in what had been internationally the most famous aspects of Borrelli's activity, namely his own work with and for street children in Naples. She was interested in this precisely *because* it had been so well known and so successful, attracting so much support and so many supporters across so many countries (not least Britain) over so many years. It was the rise and fall of such a venture that she wished to research and write about, from the point of view not merely of international voluntary action but, specifically, of the role of charismatic leadership within this. She was much less qualified—and thence less inclined—to try to unravel the politics of social action *per se* within Naples itself, or the tortuous dynamics of IPRA, or even the ramifications of the Council of Europe's expressed concern over street children.

There was of course no attempt directly to tell her what to do; nevertheless, two points of difference between researcher and researched arose early, around the very issues of hagiography and propaganda. First, the assurance that this was not to be another exercise in halo-enhancement had seemingly convinced Mario Borrelli that all earlier examples of such were to be expunged from the record (notwithstanding his own extensive library collection of the same). "I am not a saint and never have been a saint." Whereas, to the researcher, the very existence of such a body of literature—wherein Borrelli, as "saint of Naples", was routinely being compared with the likes of Mother Teresa of Calcutta—was of compelling interest. Even as late as 1985, the NATO Branch of the University of Boston (Naples Campus) was instructing certain of its students on how best to explore the lives of holy people such as Mario Borrelli (see box 1), for all that his replies to the questions asked were predictably dismissive (see box 2).

Meanwhile, and of an opposite implication from the researcher's point of view, there was what struck her as Borrelli's "propagandist" use of the language of "peace, research, education, action" to describe aspects of his own community development work. Assuredly, the very idea of community development was innovative under Borrelli's sponsorship in Naples. The experiments in alternative forms of schooling for the children of the *bassifondi*, volunteered free health services for their families, clubs and classes for women and the elderly, were all of them worthy of attention in their own right, not merely for the obvious parallels to be drawn with work being carried out in inner-city Britain with which Borrelli (thanks to his LSE experience) was familiar. Furthermore, they shed light on the ways in which what had started out as a "child rescue" venture could spawn and give way to a cluster of would-be participatory, preventive social services, thanks in this case to Borrelli's dogged determination "to get to the bottom of the problem, rather than merely keep on trying to mitigate its effects" (cf. references in Finer

---

Box 1

Coursework for "Exemplars of the Faith"

Syllabus Topic 4
Saints and holy people who are recognized as ideals towards which members of the faith should strive . . .
Questions: What makes a holy person?
a. Write a brief account of two holy people from different religions.
b. At what point in their lives did these people realise that they had a special role to fulfil and why?
c. What difficulties did they encounter in convincing other people of the truth of their message/of the value of their work?
d. Does their message/work have a continuing influence today?

Resources
The library has many books on Christian exemplars of the faith—eg Mother Teresa, Martin Luther King, Dietrich Bonhoeffer, Father Damien, **Mario Borrelli** . . .
(NATO Branch of Boston University, Naples 1985; one emphasis added)

Catherine Jones Finer

Box 2

Written replies to questions put to Borrelli by students from the NATO Branch of
Boston University (USA), 1985 (translated from the Italian by the author)

"**b**" I have never in my life felt I had a special role in respect of others, neither a sense
of mission nor a particular vocation to fulfil.

I have never accepted the idea of being a self-appointed natural leader, but simply, as
a result of being in contact with other victims of the same problems, I have accepted the
role that has been entrusted to me . . .

"**c**" The difficulties experienced were above all of a practical nature because the solution
to the problems confronting us ran contrary to local economic and political interests.
Mine was not an intellectual message. I was neither a philosopher nor a prophet. This
preoccupation for being with the weakest people stemmed naturally from a Christian
vision of life that considers every human being to be worthy of respect and endowed
with rights. Christian values had given a meaning to my existence and solidarity with
the weakest people was a natural consequence of these values . . .

These values constitute the essence of a Christian life. Putting them into practice is a
duty for every Christian; it is not heroism. To make heroes of those who put such values
into practice is a comfortable alibi for those who are not disposed to put them into
practice. Those who practise them are normal, obvious Christians. Those who do not
practise them are something else, but they are not Christians.

(Borrelli Papers 1985)

1998). It was the dressing up of such work in the promotional language of
"peace" in the writings of Borrelli and his associates of the 1970s especially
that the researcher found ideologically loaded. Witness:

> For me, and for the people who struggle to survive their hard-working
> lives, peace is a real and tangible asset, the acquisition of which makes
> our lives possible and creates real meaning. Peace seems to us such a
> controversial and unobtainable thing; it is like a mirage, always so near
> and yet so far away. It is like a toy to be played with only by the
> Olympian gods who disdain to share it with lesser mortals. But the
> seeds of violence are in the midst of our everyday lives. [Yet] if violence,
> no matter what its dimension, is able to take root in us, this also means
> that it is possible for us to regain the role of protagonists for building
> peace. To succeed in giving back to every man his role of being a
> protagonist for peace means, in fact, to put into the hands of each one
> the power to re-acquire peace. . . . (Borrelli 1997: 1)

To her mind, but not his, such material was to be accorded equivalent status
to the "hagiographic", in the sense that both should be utilized for purely
illustrative purposes.

Inevitably, there were going to be differences over the import to be at-
tached to particular words and phrases, in Italian and English. Nevertheless,
both of the above areas of difficulty stemmed as much from differences

of culture as of language. Citing examples of hagiography "for illustrative purposes" could be taken as implicit proof that the hagiography was being taken seriously—*or might be thought by others* to be being taken seriously—on its own terms. Questioning the "language of peace" could, in turn, seem like questioning the very authenticity of the commitment behind the community development work being bravely undertaken. Borrelli's "pulpit" style of writing was conspicuously more emotive and expressive, especially when translated into English, than the author felt comfortable with; just as her own style could strike him as unduly "dry British academic". In short, for all their so-called common background in applied social science, and quite apart from considerations of personal friendship, Mario Borrelli and Catherine Jones Finer were each pursuing, not so much separate agendas as separate visions of how the declared joint agenda was best to be realized and presented.

The Nature and Location of the Archive

Such considerations were compounded by questions of pure practicality, once the researcher had surveyed the archive, as initially shelved, in all its dusty length and complexity, around rooms and along corridors on the top floor of the *Fondazione Casa dello Scugnizzo* building. This was not so much "an archive" as an accumulation: of papers bound and unbound, published and unpublished, personal and impersonal, formal and informal, typed and handwritten: each in its own way a relic from Borrelli's half century of public activity. Moreover, the revealed spread of activities and interests ranged so far beyond what might have been expected as to render the author's—and especially Borrelli's—initial concerns about how best to ensure balanced coverage of the archive "as a whole" literally redundant (see box 3). Quantitative orders of magnitude were no necessary indication of anything more than the numbers and types of documents in any one field which happened to have been around at any one time, for Borrelli to have asked his helpers to store, in more—or less—formal fashion. Selection was clearly going to be of the essence. But selection on what or whose basis?

This was thus a personal archive, in the sense of its being the product of Borrelli's famed disinclination ever to discard any piece of written evidence to do with his own activities and interests, "just in case". A fair proportion of such material proved to be of such an ephemeral and chance nature (e.g. volumes of piano music to accompany contemporary Chinese popular songs, as donated by one inspired visitor to the *Casa*) as to rule itself out of the final count. No less dispensable, in this context, were shelves of works pertaining to such as the archaeology, architecture and history of Naples *per se*. Progressively more difficult to decide upon were the massive series of files on the theology of Church–State relations with special reference to Italy and thence to Naples; the vast library of documents pertaining to *gruppi spontanei* (of the 1960s) which then (some of them) became established as ongoing *gruppi volontari* in Naples; the extensive collection of unpublished papers—within-house, within-Naples and within the European (Scandinavian-led) "peace network"—numbers of which might refer to Borrelli's work

Catherine Jones Finer

Box 3

Principal contents of the archive at *Materdei*

Complete sets of the "house newspaper" *Lo Scugnizzo 1951–* , British House of Urchins Fund *Newsletter* 1961– , *Casa Dello Scugnizzo News* 1962– (i.e. the international newsletter, subsequently—1977—entitled *Materdei Community Centre*), assorted copies of French, German and Dutch newsletters.
Correspondence with Italian *benefattori*, 1950– .
Overseas correspondence, by year and country: America, Australia, Belgium, Canada, France, Germany, England (Inghilterra) (+ separate set of files for English fund-raising committee), India, Ireland, New Zealand, Netherlands (Olanda), Spain, Switzerland. [Largest section by far = England.]
Files of articles, newspaper cuttings, etc. on developments in Naples and in the Mezzogiorno generally, from 1940s on.
Documents relating to the foundation of the *Casa* (e.g. its first "action committee" complete with its own constitution) and to other groups, organizations, undertakings existing at the time and recently before.
Files on "voluntary groups" (both sociopolitical and social service-oriented) in Naples and in Italy generally, from 1960s.
Minutes of meetings held (successive series) with various other voluntary groups in Naples at *Casa dello Scugnizzo* (subsequently known as *Materdei* Community Centre).
Individual records on all boys resident at the *Casa dello Scugnizzo* 1951–1972, together with lengthy "in-house" summing-up survey report on all of them, 1972.
Social worker records, annual reports etc. on services for the elderly, for women and (variously) for children at the *Materdei* Community Centre (formerly *Casa dello Scugnizzo*) from 1972 onwards.
Records of health clinic at *Materdei* Community Centre.
Administrative records on the financial management (including sources of funds) and day-to-day running of *Casa/Materdei Centre* from 1951.
Detailed records (correspondence etc.) on relationships with the Church, locally, nationally and internationally, with particular reference to Borrelli's status as (former) priest and to ownership/status of the *Materdei* property and services (ever since 1951).
Records of *IPRI* (Italian Institute for Peace Research) since its foundation (by Borrelli *et al.*) in 1977.
Record of *Council of Europe* projects (e.g. on street children in Europe) in which Borrelli has been involved.
Borrelli's own writings: numerous papers in Italian and English, mostly unpublished; also early "autobiographical" published accounts of his work.
Books and articles about Borrelli and his work.

---

in Naples, but only usually as part of an attempt to put a broader message across.

It was also a personal archive in the sense that it included Borrelli's on-going selection of what, by implication, was to be accounted relevant (if any) *external* material for the record, from one period to the next. The most obvious source of this last in the 1950s was to be found in the pages of *Lo Scugnizzo*, the in-house-produced magazine which was famously a monthly newspaper in its own right; being rich not merely with items on the socio-economic-religious, not to say archaeological, history of Naples, but with snippets of information on what were deemed to be "*scugnizzi* types" of good work going on elsewhere in Europe, as well as with information on burgeoning foreign efforts to support the *Casa dello Scugnizzo* itself. Editions from the 1960s of *Lo Scugnizzo* (and its English-language equivalents) were, by contrast, far more exclusively concerned with reporting what, by then, was a spreading international "empire" of dedicated *Casa dello Scugnizzo* support activity. From the 1970s, by contrast again, a much reduced *Lo Scugnizzo* (down to pamphlet size in place of the original broadsheet, then tabloid size) was concentrating more or less entirely on reporting the local operational concerns and difficulties of the by now *Centro Comunitario Materdei*; albeit (in its tabloid English-language version) to what remained of an international audience.

What the archive conspicuously lacked, virtually by definition, was any sustained *independent* body of commentary on Borrelli's own activities over the entire period (other than as selected by Borrelli and/or reported in such as *Lo Scugnizzo*). For the author, within the time available to her, there seemed no way of knowing how far this dearth reflected a genuine possibility that such material had never been produced or made available, certainly within Naples; and/or how far it was evidence of a reluctance on the part of Borrelli or his staff to have such outside criticism "indiscriminately saved" for the record. On the whole, given the abundance of *inside* criticism which has precisely been stored for the record, it seems far more likely that Borrelli was never in receipt of such material, than that he took active steps to keep it out of the archive. Nevertheless, the absence of proof ensured that the compilation of a "balanced account" was not going to be entirely straightforward. For all its extensiveness, the archive at *Materdei* was critically incomplete.[3]

Nevertheless, the prime limitations of the research undertaking at the time were determined by even more immediate considerations.

On reflection, the downside of seizing on an "attractive location" is that, by definition (at least for some people), it is unlikely to be a location with which the researcher is deeply familiar or within which s/he normally operates. Furthermore, it is not necessarily going to prove equally attractive—or attractive in the same way—at all stages of the year. Climatically, for North Europeans, Naples is best experienced in spring and autumn. Winter is too cold and summer is too hot—at least given the absence of sophisticated heating and air-conditioning arrangements characteristic, as it turned out, of even a well-regulated (but economy-minded) community centre. Yet British university vacation times were fixed and there had never been any suggestion that this particular research project was worth time off from teaching.

Assuredly, the mere fact of Naples' distance from middle-England did not, of itself, render the archive inaccessible beyond the confines of the research project. However, the inconveniences of distance were compounded by the archive's cumulative changes of location: first within the top floor premises of the *Centro Comunitario Materdei* (which itself entailed extensive re-shelving activity and thence locational confusion) on Borrelli's retirement as *Presidente*; and eventually between *Materdei* and the famous—but notoriously inaccessible[4]—Naples Oratory, which Borrelli had earlier served as honorary archivist/librarian. It was this last and final move—coinciding as it did with the ending of grant aid for the project—which effectively set the seal on the operational period of this research.

For Mario Borrelli all the above was concrete proof, and thereafter a reminder, of the costs of retirement from what had otherwise been an ostensibly unpaid job. For the author as researcher, it was further confirmation of the truth that there can be no such thing as an indefinite free lunch. Paradoxically, however, she was being "saved by the bell". Given the prime need for selectivity and speed of action, the researcher was by implication acknowledged—by virtue of being left alone to get on with the job—to be the person best placed to decide on orders of priority. Whether or not this should be considered an acceptable, non-confrontational way of resolving disputes over priorities, it was certainly a convenient, practical solution.

Accordingly, the author went first for the huge body of international support correspondence (mainly in English and Italian), before tackling the entirety of *Lo Scugnizzo* publications, their English-language equivalents and the local newsletters of Borrelli's various international support groups. Next she worked through all the documentation relating to the running of, first, the *Casa*, then the *Centro Comunitario Materdei*, down to the details of the people variously involved (personalities as well as personnel), of how the monies variously raised were being spent, and of how significant others— notably of the local Church establishment—in a position to interfere, had from time to time been inclined to do just that. Everything deemed of potential significance had to be photocopied *en route* and the copies periodically transported back to England. It was a time-consuming process, with the result that there proved to be no time to wander further through the archive.

The fact that she had had only to negotiate with Borrelli over such matters was in itself significant. So far as he was concerned, the archive was his personal responsibility, about whose use no one else need in practice be consulted. Given the pronounced lack of interest in such files by the current staff of the *Centro Comunitario Materdei* (under the direction of the *Fondazione Casa dello Scugnizzo*), his stance was easy to appreciate. But this said nothing— or rather spoke volumes—about the manner in which he had been accustomed to deal with outside correspondents.

"Innocent Presences" in the Archive

Once the decision had been made to concentrate upon the international support correspondence, together with the recorded workings of the *Casa dello Scugnizzo* and its successor the *Centro Comunitario Materdei*, the researcher was in effect committed to working with what were not merely the most absorbing (for her) sections of the archive but, by the same token, the most humanly sensitive. Files of personal correspondence, arranged by country, by year, and then in alphabetical order by name, offered unrivalled insight into the functioning both of Borrelli's international "network of friends" and of their various local committees and support groups in relation to the "*Materdei* HQ". *Par excellence*, this was a collection of amateurs rather than anything approaching a professional multinational network. Very few of the key individual operators outside Naples had been trained in the niceties of management and bookkeeping, let alone in publicity and public relations *vis-à-vis* the uncommitted. Borrelli was their focus and his work their justification. This being so, there were cumulative orders of ethical dilemmas to contend with.

First, the very frankness and openness of the correspondence on record could not but raise awkward questions. Many if not most of those whose doings and opinions had been thus preserved had clearly had no notion, at the time, that they might be writing "for posterity". Many if not most of them are since deceased; though they typically have families still extant. All of them are to be presumed identifiable through this correspondence—however anonymous its citation—by anyone concerned enough to take the trouble. Not all of them or their descendants would/will presumably wish to have the actors so revealed; certainly not for the edification of a "social science readership" of no obvious, necessary relevance to them and the cause they stood for.

One particular branch of correspondence consisted of numerous reports on the efforts of various *teams* of helpers to bring groups of young people to the *Casa*, for them to stay on the premises (or as near as possible) and contribute to the quality of its life by, for instance, repainting some of its walls or even helping (1968–70) in the construction of the "New Casa" replacement building. Significantly, the correspondence is replete, not so much with appreciation of the *value* of such volunteered contributions, as of their *cost* to the supposed beneficiaries. It was not simply that paint, poorly applied, tended to fall off the walls within a short space of time, but that the teenage participants concerned—even when UN-backed—took a deal of looking after during their stay in Naples: time that local helpers could ill afford, even over the "dead" months of summer when the *Casa*'s normal inhabitants were mostly away on sponsored holidays.

Ironically, one peak of correspondence in this connection occurred over a *non*-event. Borrelli, having heard second-hand of one English school's locally advertised plan to raise money in order to travel *en masse* to the *Casa dello Scugnizzo* for the summer, suggested to the headmaster in question that it might have been simpler and cheaper all round for them to raise and send the money direct, rather than to travel themselves, especially without prior announcement to the *Casa*. The headmaster's response was revealingly tart:

> You don't seem to realize that the point of this exercise was to give our children a moving experience; not just another chance to raise money for abroad. (Borrelli Papers 1968)

So much for some of the niceties and realities of international aid, which most small-scale voluntary organizers would presumably prefer not to have advertised.

Correspondence of an even more confidential order, meanwhile, was in effect a tribute to Borrelli's charm and charisma—something which, unlike the "sainthood business", he freely admits to having made the most of for the sake of the cause ("I *enjoy* getting on with people"). In short, a smallish but steady proportion of the letters in his files, up until the later 1960s at least, were in effect veiled love letters, albeit many of them couched in terms of motherly, sisterly or daughterly love. The reactions of such correspondents to Borrelli's successive decisions to (1) spend time studying at the LSE, thus avoiding *any* outside speaking engagements over the period (1968–70); (2) change the *Casa dello Scugnizzo* into a community centre (1970); (3) seek permission to leave the priesthood (1971); and finally (4) get married (1971); might be imagined—except that there is no need to imagine, when so many of them have left their thoughts in the files of correspondence. In this case it was emphatically evident that the writers were unaware they might be contributing to "an archive"; not even when they received polite replies from Borrelli in typescript English which should have signalled, virtually by definition, that another English-language helper must have seen their letters.

Finally, and even more "personally", some of the documentation, both "in house" and between Borrelli's helpers at Naples and his committee "staff" abroad, reveals some damaging eccentricities of organization and, strikingly, of personality. Again the researcher had to grapple with problems of "exposure", this time not merely in respect of the individuals (and/or their families) concerned, but in respect of the reputation of the ongoing organization, which had only recently attained the status of *"Fondazione" Casa dello Scugnizzo*. She resolved this problem so far as the individuals were concerned, by electing only to cite material the same individuals had themselves already published. This left her with one outstanding "candidate for ignominy", now deceased but who had never, during his lifetime, displayed the smallest doubt in himself, for all his castigations of others. Witness the Rev. Bruno Scott James writing "anonymously", as usual, on the front page of *Lo Scugnizzo* of December 1959:

> To call Father Scott James Dynamic would be an understatement which he would certainly resent. Far from being a mere human dynamo, he is pure dynamite: with all its ruthless, cleansing, disruptive and leavening accompaniments . . .
>
> When he had read Morris West's *Children of the Sun* he flew out to Naples and arrived back with Don Mario Borrelli to launch an appeal for the *Casa dello Scugnizzo*. Of course he had to be in on such an adventure as this . . .
>
> He has burnt his boats in England in that attractive and wholehearted manner of his. And that compelling voice which could hold the pilgrims spellbound has the same effect despite the barriers of language and dialect on the Urchins of Naples. And that is where his friends must now go to find him.[5]

Even to repeat such *published* material can hardly be deemed helpful to the ongoing organization at *Materdei*. The only excuse, on the part of this author, could be that very few of those now involved with the *Fondazione* are likely to come across anything written in English about the *Casa* by herself. In short, this could be another "convenient solution" in the making.

Broader Churchly Perspectives and Potential Problems

The fact of Borrelli's starting off as a signed-up member of the Southern Italian Catholic Establishment—and thence of the Catholic Church world-wide—was at once a huge advantage and a huge handicap so far as the progress of his work was concerned.

Had he not been operating as a Catholic priest in Naples, the devout Australian Catholic author Morris West would almost certainly never have come to visit and then to write his famous *Children of the Sun* (West 1957) in support (and, in effect, glamorization) of Borrelli's efforts to make a difference to the lives of the postwar street children of Naples ("the most bombed city in all of Italy"). Furthermore, at least part of the subsequent growth of Borrelli's "international empire" was attributable to the response of loyal Catholic communities throughout the developed world[6] to the news of this stalwart priest with his reinvigorating message.

The researcher, however, being not herself a member of this worldwide Catholic communion, was perhaps temperamentally disinclined to take it seriously, beyond its obvious function as a generator of support and supporters—for so long as Borrelli remained a priest. Certainly she was more than ready to perceive the "downside", for Borrelli, of being on the receiving end of such an "interfering" system of international support. (The Reverend Bruno Scott James, for instance, was Morris West's own recommendation as a ready and available helper for the *Casa*: an offer which Borrelli had at the time felt it impossible to refuse.) It was only when surveying the later correspondence that she came to appreciate just how many of Borrelli's Catholic supporters had in fact stayed with him, out of sheer sympathy and friendship, after his departure from the priesthood.

Locally, by contrast, the churchly situation was characteristically more confrontational, seemingly from the start to finish of Borrelli's career. In a city of medieval hierarchical churchly tradition, Borrelli was quite simply a renegade, rebellious priest who never seemed to comprehend, or at any rate accept, that the Church had the power (1) to tell him exactly what to do, and (2) to claim full ownership of the fruits of his labours. When this last was interpreted by the then Cardinal Archbishop of Naples (1969) to mean that it was the Church which owned the newly built *Casa dello Scugnizzo* which had been financed largely through foreign fund-raising, it took the then secretary of the British Committee, writing on behalf of *all* the foreign fund-raising committees, to tell him that he was mistaken. The Cardinal Archbishop never formally acknowledged receipt of such an outlandish piece of advice; but he did nevertheless back down on the Church's claims to ownership—not least because Borrelli had in the meantime insisted that, if the Church was in truly in charge of the operation, the Church should be managing it on a day-to-day basis *forthwith* (Borrelli Papers 1969).

For the researcher, such episodes were matters primarily of curiosity and even entertainment; whereas for Borrelli they rankle still. It was a further pointed illustration of the "culture gap" between researcher and researched referred to earlier in this paper. In this particular case the gap was not merely between the believer and the non-believer or between the Catholic

Catherine Jones Finer

and the non-Catholic; but between a medieval Church-dominated southern tradition versus a modern, secular, northern, rationalist approach to the identification and analysis (albeit not necessarily to the solution!) of social problems. In short, Catherine Jones Finer was neither educationally nor, for that reason, temperamentally best equipped to explore and appreciate the convoluted Churchly dynamics of Borrelli's lifetime's experience, at home and abroad. With hindsight, this should have been an issue thought through and discussed in advance, between researcher and researched. But, out of mutual delicacy perhaps, it never was.

In Conclusion

The lessons to be drawn from this experience may be summarized as follows: To begin with, *never* turn down the chance to research an archive, if this fits in at all with your field of research experience, "style" and interest. There can be no substitute for such an enriching experience, which is likely to dominate your thinking, at least until the next archive is encountered—if, again, this continues to be your style. However, archival research being necessarily such a trusting and trusted type of activity, there are cautionary points which should ideally be observed for safety's sake from both sides, from the start.

1. Always insist on—and ideally participate in the drafting of—a detailed written agreement regarding what precisely is to be attempted, to what end.
2. Have a draft working timetable agreed in advance with every member of staff in a position to affect either the access to the archive *per se* or else access to photocopying and other facilities.
3. Reach agreement in advance on the handling of "sensitive" material: the extent to which this is to be cited and the terms on which it is to be cited.
4. Reach agreement on matters of faith/ideology: that is, on the extent to which it is or is not considered essential for the researcher to be of the same persuasion as the person(s) being researched. Obviously there are academic arguments to be put forward in favour of "dispassion" in this context; but, equally obviously, there are "insider views" which the "proprietors" of a particular research prospect may feel it necessary to ensure are represented in the eventual research report.

In short, by taking on an archive one is taking on someone else's world. It can be a wonderful, even life-changing experience. But it is not something to be taken on lightly.

Acknowledgement

The archival research referred to in this paper was funded by the Nuffield Foundation, for which the author records her thanks and her appreciation.

Appendix: Select List of Books Published in Support of Borrelli and his Work

Bodley, M. (1974), *Don Vesuvio: The Story of Father Borrelli*, London: Bachman and Turner.

Borrelli, M., with Thorne, A. (1963), *A Street Lamp and the Stars*, London: Peter Davies.

Campling, C., and Davis, M. (1970), *Words for Worship*, London: Edward Arnold.

Hargreaves, P. (1973), *Mario Borrelli*, West Yorkshire and Lindsey Regional Examination Board.

Oliver, M. (1961), An Urchin in Naples. In A. Boyle (ed.), *Heroes of Our Time*, London: Victor Gollancz.

Oliver, M. (1965), *Five Spinning Tops of Naples*, London: Dent.

Peachment, B. (1969), *The Defiant Ones*, Exeter: Religious Education Press (Pergamon).

Peachment, B. (1978), *The Tiger of Naples*, Exeter: Religious Education Press (Pergamon).

Searle, J. D. (1977), *Twentieth Century Christians*, Edinburgh: Saint Andrews Press.

West, M. (1957), *Children of the Sun*, 1st edition, London: Heinemann.

Notes

1. Award Reference SOC/100 (1478). The ESRC had also agreed to support this project but, unfortunately, even allowing for the speed of response supposed to be associated with a small grants application, the ESRC's offer of support arrived after the author's scheduled date of departure for her first episode of research in Naples.

2. For illustration of its stance and style, see Borrelli and Haavelstrud (1993).

3. The author subsequently discovered an extensive, meticulously filed collection of newspaper cuttings stored at Borrelli's family home, but this was not part of the "*Materdei* archive".

4. Owing to a mix of Naples traffic prohibitions in the vicinity and to the fact that access to the upper floor was only possible via having one of the few resident priests unlock the relevant gates, this last proved a decidedly non-functional location from the researcher's point of view.

5. It was the likes of Bruno Scott James (i.e. imported expatriate churchly helpers) who seem to have been primarily responsible for the early years of regular dismissive responses, especially to aspiring *women* helpers; assuring these that, no matter how well qualified they might think themselves to be, the *Casa dello Scugnizzo* (and indeed Naples in general) was no place for them. This from men whose only qualifications, for the most part, were that they were literate in English and trained or being trained in the mysteries of the priesthood.

6. There was even one striking letter of support and protest from a (presumably) white resident of pre-independence Zimbabwe, damning the fact that her bank accounts (in London) had all been frozen, "when there are so many more important things for the politicians of Britain and Rhodesia to be thinking about—such as the plight of the street children of Naples". Borrelli Papers.

References

Borrelli, M. (1977), Integration Between Peace Research, Peace Education and Peace Action. Unpublished paper presented to the VII General Conference of IPRA, Oaxtapec, Mexico, 11–14 December 1977.

Borrelli Papers, being the unpublished contents of the Archive in question.

Catherine Jones Finer

Borrelli, M., and Haavelstrud, M. (1993), *Peace Education Within the Archipelago of Peace Research 1945–1964*, Norway: Arena Publications, Falch Hurtingrtukk AS.

Council of Europe (1994), *Street Children*, Steering Committee on Social Policy, Study Group on Street Children, Strasbourg: Council of Europe Press.

Finer, C. Jones (1998), Transnational fundraising in a good cause: a North–South European example, *Social Policy & Administration: Special Issue on Transnational Social Policy*, 32, 5.

NATO Branch of Boston University (1985), Unpublished Coursework for 'Exemplars of the Faith', Naples: NATO.

7

Researching Homelessness and Rough Sleeping in the Scottish Context

Hilary Third

Keywords

Homelessness; Rough sleeping; Scotland

Introduction

This paper offers some reflections on a number of personal and more general issues associated with researching homelessness, particularly in the Scottish context. The paper explores a series of practical difficulties and ethical dilemmas. It also considers some of the conflicts and tensions which academic researchers face in their everyday work, in terms of the subject matter itself as well as broader questions we ask ourselves from time to time about the job that we do. In particular, it questions the justification for making a living out of researching homelessness.

The focus of my research over the past seven years has been access to social housing, specializing in homelessness and rough sleeping. During the past year I have worked on the national evaluation of the Rough Sleepers Initiative (RSI) in Scotland, and co-written a good practice guide on homelessness for the Chartered Institute of Housing in Scotland, and a review of research on homelessness in Scotland for Scottish Homes. I am currently involved in a major review of policy and practice on allocations and homelessness in England for DETR, and a study of repeat homelessness in Scotland, for Scottish Homes and Shelter (Scotland). Prior to embarking on a research career, I was an outreach worker with homeless families living in B & B. These experiences inform the personal views and reflections presented in this paper.

The main body of the paper is preceded by a short section which sets the legislative and policy context for the subject of homelessness research in Scotland.

Context

Over the past two to three years, there has been renewed vigour in the field of research on homelessness and rough sleeping. This has been stimulated in part by the activities of the Cabinet Office Social Exclusion Unit, and in particular the establishment of a Rough Sleepers Unit, under the auspices of a newly appointed "Homelessness Tsar" for England. In Scotland, there has been a focus on rough sleeping within the new Scottish Parliament. The Minister for Communities responsible for housing and homelessness in Scotland stated in a recent Parliamentary debate:

> the most extreme form of homelessness—rough sleeping—is one of the most serious forms of social exclusion in Scotland. It is demeaning, damages self-esteem and blights life chances, sometimes forever. That is why, when the First Minister invited each of his Cabinet colleagues to choose their top priority for the programme of government, I chose to end the need for anyone to have to sleep rough by the end of this Parliament. (Scottish Parliament Official Report 1999, Col. 575)

While homelessness has been incorporated within new legislation in England (Housing Act 1996), the legislative framework in Scotland has remained virtually unchanged since the 1970s. However, the Scottish policy-making framework has changed significantly with the 1999 election of the new devolved parliament. In August 1999, the Deputy Minister for Communities announced the formation of a new "homelessness task force". The task force has been charged with a remit to review the causes and nature of homelessness, examine current practice and make recommendations on strategies to tackle homelessness in Scotland (Scottish Executive News Release 1999a).

This renewed interest in homelessness in Scotland has also coincided with a housing Green Paper (Scottish Office 1999) suggesting a review of the causes and nature of homelessness—a proposal which met with widespread approval. It has also coincided with the publication of a new code of guidance on homelessness (Scottish Office 1997) and an accompanying good practice note on homelessness (Yanetta and Third 1999). Over the same period, the first Rough Sleepers Initiative (RSI) in Scotland—a national programme of funding (worth £16m from 1997 to 2000) for work with people sleeping rough—has run its course, and a second RSI (worth £20m) has been announced (Scottish Executive News Release 1999c). In total then, over the past two years, the Scottish Executive has committed more than £54m to the alleviation of homelessness, via the RSI and Empty Homes Initiatives (Scottish Executive News Release, 1999).

Despite this increased interest and activity, homelessness remains a sustained and substantial problem in Scotland. The number of households making formal homelessness presentations to Scottish local authorities reached an all-time high of 43,100 during 1997/8 (Scottish Office Statistical Bulletins HSG Series)—an increase of 5 per cent on the previous year. Visible street homelessness has also increased, and in 1999 the interim evaluation of the RSI in Scotland (Yanetta et al. 1999) established that each year, up to 11,000 individuals sleep rough in Scotland on at least one occasion.

This context has engendered a healthy demand for research. Given the interesting policy context, and the accompanying increase in research activity, it is timely to reflect upon some of the issues and dilemmas associated with conducting research on homelessness in Scotland in the 1990s and beyond. This paper first addresses some practical difficulties in researching homelessness, from definitional and methodological issues through to health and safety concerns about interviewing vulnerable people on the street. The paper then explores some more personal reflections on the ethical dilemmas which this type of work presents.

Social and Political Construction of Homelessness

Defining homelessness

One fundamental problem in researching homelessness relates to definitions. Jacobs *et al.* (1999: 11) argue that

> the definition of homelessness in Britain has changed over the last 30 years as vested interests have struggled to impose their particular inter-pretation of policy debates and to push the homelessness issue as they define it either higher up or lower down the policy agenda.

It is commonly accepted that there is a continuum of homelessness (Austerberry and Watson 1986) with "absolute homelessness" (rough sleeping) at the extreme but also including other temporary, insecure or otherwise inadequate housing arrangements. It may also be appropriate to include those *at risk of homelessness* within a broader definition, although these house-holds are even more difficult to define and identify for research purposes. Johnson *et al.*'s (1991) *Typology of Homelessness* drew on wider definitions of homelessness, suggesting that homelessness is seen as arising from an inter-related sequence of events and circumstances rather than individual events.

The United Nations definition of homelessness goes further still, suggesting that as well as people who are literally roofless, homelessness should also include:

> people whose homes do not meet UN basic standards. Those standards include adequate protection from the elements, access to safe water and sanitation, affordable prices, secure tenure and personal safety, and accessibility to employment, education and health care. (United Nations General Assembly Resolution 1984)

However, the British legislation applies a far more limited definition of homelessness—commonly described as "minimalist"—which would routinely exclude some categories of households who might be legitimately included as homeless within research studies. As Greve *et al.* (1986) suggest: "the defini-tions provided by the legislation are not alone sufficient to comprehend the nature of homelessness". Part II of the Housing (Scotland) Act 1987 defines certain types of households as "statutory homeless" and thus entitled to an offer of permanent housing by the local authority. In order to be accepted as statutory homeless, a household has to be deemed homeless or threatened with homelessness within 30 days, and in "priority need".

Priority need status is awarded to households containing dependent children, or a pregnant woman. It is also awarded to an applicant who is "vulnerable" in some other way such as old age, disability, poor physical or mental health. In addition, statutory homeless households must be judged not to have become homeless intentionally, and must usually have a local connection with the local authority to which they are applying. This relatively narrow definition means that most single homeless people are not accepted as statutory homeless and are therefore not entitled to accommodation. In short, the legislation defines who gets housed rather than who is homeless; it is not that non-priority people are not considered homeless, just that there is no obligation to house them. In a sense then, these definitions also act as mechanisms for rationing social housing, where demand exceeds supply.

National statistics on homelessness

The most significant national data source on homelessness in Scotland is the quarterly return which each local authority makes to the Scottish Executive detailing all the cases it has dealt with under the homeless persons legislation. This form (HL1) records details of individual cases, in terms of (for example) household characteristics, causes of homelessness and outcome of the local authority's decision, as well as the accommodation or other assistance provided.

While HL1 is a valuable source of data it has certain shortcomings. First, the form records details of homeless *presentations*, rather than incidence of homelessness. Many households do not approach the local authority when they become homeless, either because they do not know their rights, or because they know that they would be considered "non-priority" under the terms of the legislation and thus not entitled to rehousing. For these reasons, the figures represent only a partial picture of homelessness. Second, Evans *et al.*'s (1994) detailed research on the operation of the 1991 Code of Guidance on homelessness in Scotland identified inconsistency in the way that local authorities implement the homelessness legislation and how they record their activities in the statistical returns to the Scottish Office, which casts further doubt on the reliability of HL1 data.

Third, the impact of organizational structures of local authorities, and the way in which the homelessness duty is delivered has a significant effect on the homelessness statistics. Accordingly, earlier work by the author (Third 1993) suggested that understanding the structures and processes within which an authority administers homelessness duties enables us to interpret and understand the statistics, and that although the limitations of the homelessness statistics are widely acknowledged, they continue to form the basis for research into the implementation of the homelessness legislation. Arguing that it is necessary to move away from the use of the official statistics if we are to understand the implementation of the legislation, the author concludes that

a commitment to homelessness research necessitates discarding the
traditional methods and assumptions, and developing a more rigorous
approach . . . taking into account the difficulties emanating from all stages
of the policy/action process. (1993: 97)

Quantifying rough sleeping

There are a number of obvious difficulties in researching the extent of rough
sleeping (see, for example, Yanetta *et al.* 1999). There are significant limitations
to any "head count" method (searches for people sleeping rough on a chosen
night usually in town/city centres targeted known sites for rough sleeping),
particularly in rural and semi-rural areas, and during the winter.

Indeed, Shelter (Scotland) who coordinated a number of head counts and
"hostel vacancy audits" (to assess whether there is sufficient capacity to meet
the local need for hostel-type accommodation) for local authorities preparing
RSI bids, readily acknowledges this method to be inadequate. Any examination of rough sleeping in Scotland, particularly outside of the main conurba-
tions, is made more difficult if there are no emergency hostels, resettlement
units or day centres through which to contact rough sleepers, or conduct
"vacancy audits".

Furthermore, research on the extent and nature of homelessness in Tayside (Webb *et al.* 1994) concluded that many people who are forced to sleep
rough, particularly in rural areas, take great care to keep their "skippers"
secret, making themselves not only less vulnerable to attack, but also hiding
themselves from Census enumerators and other researchers. Given that rough
sleeping tends to be *ad hoc*, often for a few nights between staying with friends
or living "care of" various addresses, it is not surprising that snapshot head
counts undercount the true extent of rough sleeping. It will also fail to count
young people known to "sleep out" in peripheral housing estates. Webb *et al.*
conclude that

> providing accurate estimates [is] problematic and there is an important
> need to develop recording and monitoring procedures to generate more
> robust figures. (1994: vii)

The 1991 Census for the first time attempted to include people who were
without a home and sleeping rough. Across the UK, 2,845 people sleeping
rough were identified; 145 in Scotland. Both figures were widely acknowledged to underestimate the true extent of street homelessness. Oldman and
Halton (1993), writing on the failure of the Census to measure the extent of
rough sleeping, argue that the results of the inappropriate head count method
gave a false impression of the extent and nature of the problem. First, it
implied that the problem was relatively small and only occurred in any
significant proportion in central London. This in turn led to inadequate
funding which was targeted solely on central London, to the exclusion of the
rest of the UK where smaller numbers of people sleeping out (or none at all)
had been identified on Census night. However, they also argue that reliance

Hilary Third

on a snapshot enumeration of people sleeping out leads to a dangerous tendency to equate street homelessness with single homelessness, and that

> in effect, the government's agenda with regard to single homeless people has been based on a narrow definition of the problem as one of rooflessness. (Oldman and Halton 1993: 1)

Similar issues have been raised in the Scottish Parliament, with the Scottish National Party's spokesperson on housing voicing concern that "the debate on homelessness has centred solely around the issue of rooflessness" (Scottish Parliament Official Report, September 1999, col. 580). Oldman and Halton (1993) suggest that this obscures the fact that people sleeping rough represent only a small percentage of single homeless people when compared with numbers living in hostels, B & B, staying with friends or living in a range of other temporary and precarious housing arrangements. These methods also fail adequately to identify women and minority ethnic groups whose homelessness tends to be more concealed (Webb, 1994).

Other methods have been used to try to estimate the extent of "absolute homelessness" in Scotland. Research for the Scottish Office, for example, attempted to estimate the prevalence of rooflessness over a six-month period by adopting a "contact-recontact" method frequently used in field ecology studies, and increasingly in health and homelessness studies in the UK, USA and Australia. The study was not successful in its main objective, and a number of reasons for this are suggested, including refusal of agencies and clients to participate, time constraints and ethical concerns, as well as difficulties of using the method to estimate national rather than local populations. In short, the research provided a wealth of interesting observations about the methodological problems of counting roofless people, but because of these problems it was unable to present figures for the prevalence of rooflessness in Scotland (Shaw et al. 1996).

The latest attempt to quantify rough sleeping in Scotland (described in Yanetta et al. 1999) used a range of methods to estimate that between 8,400 and 11,000 individuals slept rough in Scotland on at least one occasion during the year 1997/8. The principal method used to reach this estimate had been piloted in a range of other research studies around Scotland, producing robust estimates which were widely accepted as realistic at the local level (Yanetta et al. 1997a; Housing Plus 1999; Yanetta et al. 1994; Webb et al. 1994; Third and Yanetta 1998). This involved seeking information (through short questionnaires, face-to-face interviews, and analysis of records) to identify the proportion of single homeless people who had slept rough during the previous year, and applying this to the number of single people presenting to the same local authority as homeless during the same year (data drawn from HL1 statistical returns to the Scottish Executive).

For the national estimate, five local studies (in East Lothian, Highland, Kirkcaldy, Tayside and North and South Ayrshire) which found that the proportion of single homeless people who had slept rough ranged from 33 to 43 per cent were applied to the 43,000 single people applying to Scottish local authorities as homeless in 1997/8. However, this national estimate—

while higher than any previous estimates—is still likely to be an underestimate, as many single homeless people are not recorded in official homelessness statistics because they do not approach the local authority when they become homeless. This is unsurprising given the limited assistance to which they are entitled under the terms of the legislation. The two supplementary methods used to substantiate the principal method are described in the report of the evaluation of the RSI (Yanetta *et al.* 1999). The national estimate, announced in the Scottish Parliament in September 1999, was accepted by all parties. It has subsequently been widely quoted, particularly as justification for increased funding and activity around homelessness in Scotland. However, it is important that there is not a preoccupation with quantifying the problem, which obscures the need to understand and resolve it.

Practical and Ethical Issues in Researching Homelessness

Homeless people are—almost by definition—a highly mobile group which is consequently difficult to identify and contact for research purposes. Local authority records are often unreliable and in any case only include those people who have approached the authority. Records cannot therefore be depended upon as a method of quantifying, or identifying homeless people to interview.

An alternative method of contacting homeless people is through agencies providing accommodation or services. Admittedly, this introduces the possibility of bias as those who are in contact with a particular service may be different in a significant way from those who have failed to make contact with the service, or who have been excluded from it. When gathering a sample of homeless people in this way it is difficult to avoid bias, because the researcher often depends upon the service provider to identify potential clients to interview.

In studying homelessness there are dilemmas not only about how to identify and contact the respondent, but also about the point at which to conduct an interview. For example, conducting interviews at the point of actual homelessness involves interacting with an individual in crisis, which may be considered insensitive or unreasonable. On the other hand, to wait until the homelessness is resolved might introduce other difficulties of losing the prospective respondent. Some American studies have used "tracking" techniques to overcome this problem (Cohen *et al.* 1993) but such methods rely upon the respondent maintaining contact with certain services, and have heavy resource implications. This may render such methods impractical in the British context of homelessness services.

There is also an issue as to whether it is preferable to study homelessness from a longitudinal or retrospective approach. There are clearly merits and limitations associated with both approaches. A significant advantage of a retrospective approach, for example, is that it will generate findings relatively quickly, compared with a longitudinal approach. It would also benefit from being able to identify from the outset individuals who are the main focus of the study, whereas under a longitudinal approach it would be necessary to identify and "follow" a broad cross-section of applicants over a period. On the other hand, a longitudinal study would have the advantage of tracing particular households through the homelessness and rehousing procedure, and monitoring their longer-term housing outcomes. However, such an approach might prove relatively expensive, as well as time-consuming.

There are significant practical problems involved in the retrospective methodology, for example in identifying an adequate sample of applicants with whom to conduct interviews. While it may be possible to access local authority records to carry out statistical analyses, data protection restrictions effectively rule out their use as a means of identifying individuals who might be eligible for inclusion as interviewees. In order to comply with the legislation it would be necessary to ask local authorities or other landlord agencies (such as housing associations) to write to applicants seeking their permission to release their contact details to a research team, and unless some form of incentives are offered, this might not produce a significant (or reliably representative) return.

Another limitation of a retrospective approach is that it relies upon respondents' memories and ability to recall details, which may be particularly difficult in relation to the more chaotic lifestyles of some homeless people. Furthermore, local authority practice in relation to housing and homelessness may change over time such that, in a sense, the research is evaluating outdated practice. Indeed, it is to be hoped that the publication of good practice guidance on homelessness (Yanetta and Third 1999) will have given recent impetus to such changes.

There are other useful research methods which do not involve contacting homeless people directly. For example, one way of "testing" the implementation and outcome of homelessness policies is through the use of "cameos" of hypothetical applicants. More commonly known as "vignettes", these provide a method for "standardized evaluation of the nature of agency responses in various settings and dealing with different kinds of clients" (Bannister *et al.* 1993). This method is to be employed in the ongoing study of homelessness, allocations and transfers for DETR and was found to be highly successful in earlier Scottish research (Yanetta *et al.* 1997b). It overcomes some of the problems of client confidentiality and data protection and can be an efficient tool for gathering comparable data to enable the identification of similarities and differences in practice.

Difficulties in setting and meeting interview targets with homeless people

Homelessness research often involves a fairly complex sampling frame, with targets that can be difficult to achieve. For example, the survey of service users conducted for the Scottish RSI evaluation (Yanetta *et al.* 1999) involved drawing a balanced sample according to a number of set criteria. However, although good planning is essential for successful fieldwork, there may be factors beyond the control of the interviewer which may make it difficult to achieve targets. For example, interviewers accompanied outreach workers from an Edinburgh-based project on two separate streetwork shifts, with a target of conducting a total of twelve interviews. Most unusually—and apparently inexplicably—no homeless people were identified during either session and the project had to be excluded from the survey. In order to maintain the agreed balance within the sample, a similar project in another area had to be contacted at short notice and persuaded to participate in the research so as to ensure that users of outreach/streetwork projects were adequately represented. Fortunately, interviews in the other projects were achieved without difficulty, and overall targets were exceeded.

Interviewers sometimes had difficulties in reaching target numbers. One team spoke of how their visit to a particular area coincided with a visit of a well-known local drug dealer, which led to many of the potential respondents vanishing from their usual "pitches". Another team ran into difficulties because their session with the outreach workers for some evening streetwork coincided with a major televised football match, which meant it was difficult to find and then persuade people to be interviewed that night.

Despite a desire to meet interview targets, the researcher always has to put the needs of the respondent first. Tempting though it may be, it is unwise and unethical to pursue potential respondents, or to interview them against their will, or in inappropriate circumstances. It is essential to cause minimal disruption for agencies working with homeless people. Meeting interview targets is unimportant in the context of the needs of the homeless person, or the work the agency/service is attempting to carry out. The researcher has a moral responsibility to maintain good relationships with agencies and their clients, and to treat them with sensitivity and respect in all situations. This must be a founding principle in conducting research with homeless people, and those who provide accommodation and services to them.

Health and safety: reducing the risks

Interviews with homeless people can be extremely harrowing. Respondents are often in crisis, and many have additional challenging problems. Most interviews will necessarily involve exploring the causes and/or consequences of an individual's homelessness, which can involve tackling extremely sensitive issues. Market research companies may be unwilling to take on such complex and specialized work, particularly if interviews are likely to take place in hostels or even on the street, often out of hours. Using senior postgraduate housing students—fully trained and properly supported—for such interviews has proved extremely successful in a number of Scottish studies of homelessness (for example Yanetta *et al.* 1999; Yanetta *et al.* 1997b). It has also provided students with valuable relevant experience for future employment.

It is considered good practice within universities and other organizations to carry out risk assessments for various tasks and to have regard to health and safety guidelines. There is a perception that the risks of interviewing homeless people—particularly on the street or in hostels—is higher than with other interviewees. Is this a manifestation of prejudice, or is this indeed a "dangerous" group? Certainly, there is a prevalence of mental ill-health, as well as drug and alcohol use amongst the street-homeless population, which carries with it certain increased risks. Obviously, researchers should exercise common sense, but also have to show some trust and perhaps take some (calculated) risks in order to show respect for the respondent, and thus do justice to the research.

In conducting interviews with homeless people in Scotland, a number of practical steps were taken to reduce the risks. First, interviewers worked in pairs and ensured that they were never out of earshot of their partner. The survey coordinator had agreed a programme of interviews with each RSI project, and thus knew the precise location of each team at all times. Each team was provided with a mobile phone, and was given strict instructions to ring the survey coordinator at four agreed times per day. A set of procedures were in place to take action if the expected phone calls were not received at the agreed times.

Pre-fieldwork preparation included basic risk assessment and procedures. In particular, the importance of conducting interviews in a safe environment with a clear exit, and the importance of ending an interview if feeling threatened, were emphasized. In case of emergency, each interviewer was provided with an attack alarm, and instructed on its use. In addition, the interviewers were fully trained prior to going out in the field, and received ongoing support throughout the fieldwork period.

However, it would be wrong to overstate the difficulties and risks in researching homelessness. Interviewing people who are without shelter can also be one of the most humbling and positive experiences within a research career.

Making a career out of homelessness

A series of articles in the media and in the housing press in late 1999 has revealed a controversial view that some professional and voluntary action on homelessness may be misguided, or counterproductive. In an interview in the *Observer* (14 November 1999) for example, Louise Casey, appointed as the government's "Homelessness Tsar" in February 1999, criticized the well-meaning but misdirected "culture of kindness", which she blamed for keeping homeless people on the streets, and argued that the "homelessness industry" should be dismantled. It is clear that there *is* a homelessness "industry" in Scotland, as elsewhere in Britain, particularly (but not exclusively) in urban areas. A significant number of individuals make a career out of homelessness—whether as policy makers, campaigners, practitioners, or in this case as researchers.

It could therefore be argued that there is a homelessness *research* industry. In a number of housing-based research centres around the country, homelessness and related issues account for a significant proportion of income, which not only contributes to the financial well-being of the institution in question, but also helps to ensure that fixed-term contracts of research staff are renewed. From a personal perspective, almost all my own contract research activity for the past and coming year focuses on homelessness, bringing substantial income to the institution. Certainly then, research into homelessness in Scotland is a thriving business.

An important ethical dilemma relates to the researcher's role within this homelessness industry. Sensitive researchers must come to terms with the uncomfortable truth that they are making a living out of poverty and social exclusion. Such dilemmas are brought into sharp focus when a researcher during an interview with a homeless person is confronted with questions such as: "Have *you* ever been homeless?" "What kind of home do you live in?" "How much do you get paid for researching homelessness?" These are uncomfortable and embarrassing questions to answer.

Is there a need for any more homelessness research?

Research often raises more questions than it answers, and many studies on homelessness include recommendations for further research. It is clearly in the interests of participants in the research and homelessness industries to recommend more research, thereby perpetuating the industry and protecting our own jobs. This raises a serious question: How far are those who are part of the industry and make a living out of research capable of making an objective decision about whether or not there needs to be more research in their field?

First, it is clear that the academic community does not bear sole responsibility for making this decision. In the increasingly market-oriented research environment (even in the field of homelessness) there has been a shift towards responding to preset research programmes and evaluating short-term policy initiatives rather than seeking funding to respond to our own research priorities. Perhaps academics should resist opportunities to become involved in such research, but this is clearly more difficult in a competitive environment where core funding has declined and there is increased pressure to meet the costs of all research from external sources. If the lion's share of research funding is channelled through preset research agendas to which academics and other researchers have limited input, then control rests with governmental and other organizations who may have their own agendas influencing decisions about areas for funded research. Responding to invitations to tender for such work—even if privately researchers do not feel it is necessarily valuable—amounts to colluding with those agendas in order to secure our jobs.

A recent review of major research on homelessness in Scotland (Third and Yanetta 2000) listed more than fifty separate studies published since 1990. The review concluded that while there were some research gaps in homelessness in the Scottish context (such as the experience of homelessness amongst older people, ethnic minorities and women), other issues (such as youth homelessness) tended to be over-researched. Perhaps there has been enough research. On the other hand, new research can provide new insights. Furthermore, the context for homelessness is in constant flux and may change over time and space, necessitating more research. This suggests an almost infinite capacity for research, but the issue remains about comparative benefits arising from research for the "subjects".

There have also been situations wherein two organizations fund similar research, focusing upon the same client group; lack of communication—or inability to work effectively together—may mean that funding (often drawn from the public purse) is being wasted. Indeed, the two principal funders of Scottish housing research (Scottish Homes and the Scottish Executive) currently run separate research programmes, although this will change as Scottish Homes is merged with the Executive, as announced in December

1999 (Scottish Executive News Release 1999d). This suggests there is a need for the research community—funders and contractors—to work more closely together. However, the competitive tendering process tends to work against the spirit of cooperation amongst different research teams as well as different organizations working with homeless people in a particular local area.

Conflicting demands

There are currently significant pressures on researchers within universities— even those involved predominantly or exclusively on contract research— to focus on work which will lead to academic outputs rated highly by the Research Assessment Exercise (RAE). Herein lies a conflict. Contract research—particularly in very practice-based work around homelessness— may not necessarily lend itself to academic publications. However, these may be the commissions which influence housing practice, and therefore offer the most scope to be of real benefit to homeless people.

A recent example is the good practice guide on homelessness written for the Chartered Insitute of Housing in Scotland (Yanetta and Third 1999). The practice note has been well received amongst practitioners working within the field of homelessness, and has already warranted a second print run. However, despite its clear importance and relevance to the world of practice, such publications are not academic peer-reviewed and therefore do not rank highly in RAE terms. On the other hand, research institutions which also run vocational courses leading to Chartered Institute of Housing validated qualification must be involved in such work in order to retain credibility with local housing agencies who sponsor their staff to take these courses. Undertaking such practice-based studies has the additional benefit of enabling staff to provide up-to-date, relevant teaching. There is a strong argument that the RAE assessment does not reflect the real world of contract research which is carried out in many universities today, particularly within social policy.

Arguably, if homelessness research is justifiable, it has to contribute to policy and/or practice developments. To study homeless people out of aca-demic curiosity is no more defensible than to undertake research simply to keep ourselves employed. On the other hand, there is clearly a need to explore the complexities of homelessness so as to understand the problem in order to deal with it effectively. There may be a conflict between under-taking research which is acceptable to homeless people and those who work with them, as well as the academic community.

As well as academic pressures, there are also financial pressures within academic institutions and the contract culture, and this too impinges on research. Homelessness research is contracted in a highly competitive mar-ket environment. In Scotland alone, there are more than a dozen research institutions (within universities and private consultancies) who regularly bid for work in this field. Some research commissioners routinely under-cost research, and as long as researchers are prepared to take on under-funded contracts this situation will persist. All too often, conscientious researchers exceed contracted time in order to submit a respectable piece of work. This only makes it more difficult to reconcile other pressures such as teaching, writing academic articles and responding to "invitations to tender" for new research studies. It has long been stated that higher education runs on good will. Perhaps that is true also of research in applied social policy.

The consequences of research in homelessness

When research is around an issue which so directly affects the quality of life of individuals living in our communities, questions as to whether research actually does any good become particularly poignant. Aside from this central question, there is also the possibility that research can also bring about some unintended and undesirable consequences, for which the researcher may then feel in some way responsible.

For example, research can uncover benefit fraud which the researcher may feel uncomfortable about reporting. A recent example comes from research amongst rough sleepers in Scotland (Yanetta *et al.* 1999) which identified a high level of illicit drug use and involvement with the criminal justice system. This is clearly an important finding which has implications for policy and practice responses, but raises dilemmas for researchers about how to present such facts, as well as fears about what impact this may have subsequently on the way homeless people are perceived and treated. In a worst-case scenario, the media might present the research as branding homeless people "criminals" or "junkies" or both. This can negatively impact on the public's will to help if research fuels a perception that homeless people can be blamed for their predicament. Where research identifies sensitive issues, there are questions for the researcher wishing to operate in the best interests of the client group, while still maintaining objectivity in presenting research findings.

Another important question relates to the role of the researcher in ensuring that research is properly disseminated, so that it at least has the *potential* to influence policy and practice. Clearly, *implementation* of research recommendations is (usually) beyond the control of the researcher and often rests with the commissioning body, or with elected politicians. It may be difficult for the researcher to exert any influence at all on how the research is handled after completion of the contract, particularly if the client holds the copyright. This raises other related questions about the appropriate relationships between researchers, funders and the policy process, and the implications which interorganizational relationships have for the credibility of independent academic research.

Perhaps researchers could assist the implementation process by considering how to make research more user-friendly, as well as improving dissemination strategies. Dissemination of research is often neglected, either because it is not funded, or more commonly, because as soon as one research contract is completed, other deadlines are looming. Indeed, it is not unusual for a contract researcher to be working on four or five separate research contracts at any one time.

Failure to make effective use of completed research is a serious issue, particularly when it concerns the welfare of homeless people. However, most commissioners do not fund the researcher to undertake dissemination, and often fail to disseminate adequately themselves. In such cases, one of the most important parts of the research process is being neglected and there is a danger that the research fails to influence policy or practice.

There is an argument for providing special funding for dissemination and secondary analysis of existing research, alongside (or instead of) more primary research. Such a unit focusing on housing and homelessess research could be set up along the lines of the NHS Centre for Reviews and Dissemination (CRD) within the Institute for Research in Social Science at University of York. Established in 1994, The CRD, by offering rigorous and systematic reviews on selected topics, a database of good quality reviews and a dissemination service, is helping to promote research-based practice in the NHS (http://www.york.ac.uk/inst/crd/centre.htm).

User involvement in research (and policy development) in homelessness

In an increasingly market-oriented environment, service users (even in the public sector) are being viewed as customers, with choices. Despite the "Investors in People" scheme, and "Citizen's Charter", social housing is not as good as other services at providing a "customer-focused" approach, and still tends to be something which is "done unto" applicants. There is a growing interest in increasing choice in the allocations process (particularly in the English context) as a way of improving the sustainability of tenancies and communities, but in Scotland this has received little attention to date.

For homeless people this tends to be even more the case, as they are too often seen as supplicants. This is particularly true for vulnerable homeless people, many of whom have additional needs. There is currently a lack of user involvement in policy development in this field. Research has a role to play in user involvement but there is a need to explore the potential for this.

It is considered good practice—a basic courtesy—to ensure that participants in social research are provided with feedback. Indeed, a common approach is to send copies of a research report or summary of findings to interviewees. While this may be a relatively straightforward procedure in most research studies, it is much harder for research in which respondents are a highly mobile group. There is consequently a danger that respondents in homelessness research will feel that nothing ever came of the study to which they contributed. This in turn contributes to an apathy about research, which serves to disempower homeless people still further. Given the government's current interest in social exclusion, this would seem to be an ideal time to consider involvement of such a marginalized group, not only in responding to research, but also—in a more significant way—involvement in the policy process.

The Deputy Minister for Communities, chairing the first meeting of the Homelessness Task Force in Glasgow, said that the Task Force gave homeless people a real opportunity to help shape government policy:

Our work will be guided by the real experts—those with direct experience of homelessness. Today, Task Force members are listening to *Big Issue* vendors. In the coming months we will hear a range of other homeless people's views on the way forward. (Scottish Executive News Release 1999b)

Similarly, in the debate in the Scottish Parliament (16 September 1999) she stated that

it is important that we not only understand the problems and identify practical measures to address them, but listen to homeless people, as, frankly, they are the real experts. (Scottish Parliament Official Report 1999: col. 600)

Despite the significant resources which have already been allocated to homelessness and rough sleeping in Scotland, no funds have been specifically earmarked to initiatives to explore and encourage user involvement in the interlinked processes of research, policy and practice. Whether "participation", "empowerment" and "user involvement" go beyond the rhetoric of the Homelessness Task Force, or the Scottish Social Inclusion Network, remains to be seen. Certainly, there is a dearth of specific guidance (or good practice examples) about how to involve users in the planning and provision of policy and services in a meaningful way, and any progress in this area is long overdue.

Conclusions

The terms "industry" and "business" have pejorative overtones when applied to homelessness, suggesting an exploitative relationship with homeless people. In defence, the research community might wish to argue that research is not exploitative where it contributes directly to increasing the well-being or improving the prospects of homeless people. Research clearly plays a role in improving understanding of the causes and nature of homelessness, and a plethora of recent studies (see for example Third and Yanetta 2000; Fitzpatrick *et al.* 2000) have made a valuable contribution to exposing the extent of homelessness, and the extremely complex variety of processes which cause homelessness. This provides potential justification for the existence of "an industry'; it is the effectiveness of this industry in tackling homelessness which requires closer examination. Unless research is translated into effective policy and practice responses, then there is no justification for the perpetuation of the industry.

Researchers in the field of homelessness occupy a privileged position, at best providing a link between homeless people and frontline agencies, and policy makers. At worst, they make a living out of poverty and social exclusion, without making an adequate contribution to understanding and alleviating those problems.

This paper has reflected upon a number of ethical and practical issues associated with research in this one area of applied social policy. In taking a candid look at some of the difficulties, it has attempted to contribute to improving the approach to research in this important area. Homelessness is not an easy issue to research; it is littered with methodological and other obstacles, and researchers have made well-documented mistakes. The challenge—and opportunity—for the future is to learn from these mistakes, and build on past experiences to improve the quality of the work that we produce.

Acknowledgements

This paper draws heavily on work conducted jointly with a number of other researchers, particularly Anne Yanetta and Hal Pawson at the School of Planning and Housing, ECA/Heriot-Watt University, and Isobel Anderson at Stirling University. Thank you for being such good collaborators. I am grateful to friends and colleagues for providing encouragement and helpful comments on the draft of this paper. Most of all, I need to thank my office mate Heidi Rettig, without whom this paper would not have been written at all.

References

Austerberry, H., and Watson, S. (1986), *Housing and Homelessness: A Feminist Perspective*, London: Routledge and Kegan Paul.

Bannister, J., Dell, M., Donnison, D., Fitzpatrick, S., and Taylor, R. (1993), *Homeless Young People in Scotland: The Role of the Social Work Services*, Edinburgh: HMSO.

Cohen, E. H., Mowbray, C. T., Bybee, D., Yeich, S., Ribisl, K., and Freddolino, P. (1993), Tracking and follow-up methods for research on homelessness, *Evaluation Review*, 17, 3, June: 331–52.

Evans, R., Smith, N., Bryson, C., and Austin, N. (1994), *The Operation of the 1991 Code of Guidance on Homelessness in Scotland*, Edinburgh: Scottish Office Central Research Unit.

Fitzpatrick, S., Kemp, P., and Klinker, S. (2000), *A Review of Single Homelessness Research in Britain*, York: Joseph Rowntree Foundation and CRASH.

Greve, J., Groves, R., Murie, A., and Watson, L. (1986), *Homelessness in London (Working Paper 60)*, University of Bristol, SAUS.

Housing Plus (1999), *The Incidence of Rough Sleeping and Homelessness in the Highlands*, Report for the Highland Council and Highland Health Board.

Jacobs, K., Kemeny, J., and Manzi, T. (1999), The struggle to define homelessness: a constructivist approach. In S. Hutson and D. Clapham (eds), *Homelessness: Public Policies and Private Troubles*, London.

Johnson, B., Murie, A., Naumann, L., and Yanetta, A. (1991), *A Typology of Homelessness*, Edinburgh: Scottish Homes.

Oldman, J., and Halton, S. (1993), *The Numbers Game. Lessons from Birmingham. The Failure of the 1991 Census to Measure People Sleeping Rough*, London: CHAR.

Property People (1999), Apologise or Quit, Charity Tells Casey, 214, 18 November.

Scottish Executive News Release (1999a), SE1230/99, 17 June.

Scottish Executive News Release (1999b), SE0401/99, 25 August.

Scottish Executive News Release (1999c), SE1250/99, 10 November.

Scottish Executive News Release (1999d), SE1626, December.

Scottish Office (1997), *Code of Guidance on Homelessness*, 3rd edn, Edinburgh: Scottish Office.

Scottish Office (1999), *Investing in Modernization: An Agenda for Scotland's Housing*, Green Paper, Edinburgh: Scottish Office.

Scottish Parliament Official Report (1999), vol 2, no. 6, 16 September.

Shaw, I., Bloor, M., and Roberts, S. (1996), *Estimating Rooflessness in Scotland*, Edinburgh: Scottish Office Central Research Unit.

The Observer (1999), *Sweep the Homeless off Streets*, 14 November.

Third, H. (1992), *Home Truths: A Study of Family Homelessness in Thanet*, London: Children's Society.

Third, H. (1993), *Responding to Homelessness: An Alternative Study of Local Authority Practice*. Unpublished MA Dissertation, University of York.

Third, H., and Yanetta, A. (1998), *Homelessness and Rough Sleeping in N&S Ayrshire*. Unpublished Research Report.

Third, H., and Yanetta, A. (2000), *Homelessness in Scotland: A Review of Major Research Since 1990*, Edinburgh: Scottish Homes.

Webb, S. (1994), *My Address is not My Home: Hidden Homelessness and Single Women in Scotland*, Edinburgh: SCSH/GCSH.

Webb, S., Edwards, L., Murie, A., and Yanetta, A. (1994), *The Nature, Extent and Experience of Homelessness in Tayside*, Edinburgh: School of Planning and Housing, ECA/Heriot-Watt University.

Yanetta, A., and Third, H. (1999), *Homelessness in Scotland: A Good Practice Note*, Edinburgh: Chartered Institute of Housing in Scotland.

Yanetta, A., Edwards, L., Dickie, J., and Stevens, C. (1994), *Youth Homelessness in Kirkcaldy District*, Kirkcaldy: Kirkcaldy District Council.

Yanetta, A., Third, H., and Anderson, I. (1999), *National Monitoring and Interim Evaluation of the Rough Sleeper's Initiative in Scotland*, Edinburgh: Scottish Executive.

Yanetta, A., Third, H., and Lomax, D. (1997a), *Homelessness and Rough Sleeping in East Lothian*. Unpublished Research Report.

Yanetta, A., Third, H., and Butler, H. (1997b), *Feasibility of a Common Housing Register in the West End of Glasgow*. Unpublished research report.

8

Researching Risk in the Probation Service

Hazel Kemshall

Keywords

Risk; Research; Ethics

The Context of Ethical and Political Dilemmas in Offender Risk Research

Barnes (1979: 16) has stated that ethical decisions

> arise when we try to decide between one course of action and another not in terms of expediency or efficiency but by reference to standards of what is morally right or wrong.

Such dilemmas can influence two sets of decisions:

- how to carry out the research (in effect the principles of operation);
- how research findings should be disseminated and applied.

However, standards of "what is morally right or wrong" are rarely clear-cut. Punch (1986: 12) has argued that such dilemmas "often have to be resolved situationally . . . without the chance of armchair reflection", and that research is also prone to political processes. These can range from the "micropolitics of personal relationships" to the powerful influence of government departments and the "state itself" (Punch 1986: 12). According to Broadhead (1982):

> Absolute ethical standards, oblivious to political and class realities, are fundamentally at odds with the irreverent attitude necessary to ask difficult questions, observe difficult situations, and substantiate findings with dispassion. (1982: 121)

Ethical and political difficulties are particularly severe in areas where the research is focused on politically sensitive issues or where they are topical and likely to attract media attention (Sieber and Stanley 1988). In such situations the researcher is likely to be exposed to severe pressure from policy makers, politicians and funders to produce research which uncritically promotes policy-driven ends. The assessment and management of risk in penal policy has arguably been one of the most politically sensitive research topics of the 1990s, particularly the identification and assessment of risky and dangerous offenders. Such sensitivity has been exacerbated by the "politicization of risk" in the risk society, and the increasing centrality of risk concerns to social and penal policy.

The rise of risk in penal policy and the risk society

Commentators such as Beck (1992) and Giddens (1990, 1991) have noted the rise of the "risk society". Beck has argued that we are moving from a society concerned with the distribution of goods to one concerned with the distribution of risks. Beck argues that access to and control over goods is now less important than inequitable and undesirable exposure to risks. According to Beck, in societies concerned with the distribution of goods the focus of concern is with the substantive and positive goals of social change, with attempts to ensure equity for all and the communal good (Kemshall *et al.* 1997: 223). However, the concerns of risk society are peculiarly defensive, concerned with risk avoidance and protection from harm. The axial principle of risk society is not the equitable distribution of "goods" but the distribution and avoidance of hazards, dangers and risks (Beck *et al.* 1994). As Lupton expresses it: "Debates and conflicts over risks have begun to dominate public, political and private arenas" (1999: 59). This has been accompanied by a growing public scepticism of expert knowledge (Irwin and Wynne 1996; Wynne 1982, 1989; Grove-White 1998) and distrust in conflicting expert knowledge systems (Wynne 1996), epitomized by the *E. coli* and BSE (bovine spongiform encephalopathy) crises in the UK.

Whilst Beck and Giddens have been concerned with the "high-consequence risks" arising from industrialization and globalization (Petersen 1996: 45), social care, health and crime risks have not been immune to such risk preoccupations (Alaszewski *et al.* 1998; Bloor 1995a, 1995b; Kemshall 1998a; Kemshall and Pritchard 1996, 1997). Penal policy interest in offender risk assessment, whilst not a new phenomenon (Bottoms 1977), has increased throughout the 1990s (Kemshall 1996a, 1998a).[1] This has been particularly acute in respect of sexual and dangerous offenders (Home Office 1997a, 1997b, 1998, 1999; Home Office Circular 39 (1997); Kemshall 2000), fuelled by media attention and public concern in individual cases (for example the murder of Jamie Bulger). The emphasis has been upon the accurate prediction of levels of risk, most notably for the safe release of prisoners into the community and for the effective identification and regulation of offenders in the community (Kemshall 1997, 1998a; Kemshall *et al.* 1997). In this context the research agenda has largely been policy-driven, determined by the agenda of central policy makers (e.g. the Home Office, the Department of Health), and used to produce structured assessment tools (such as LSIR and OASYS) to "guide" or supplement professional judgement (Roberts *et al.* 1996).

Hazel Kemshall

Research and normative assumptions

Such research uncritically adopts the normative definitions of risk provided by central policy makers and managers, and is usually informed by a desire to rationalize existing services and increase the accountability of professionals (Clarke *et al.* 1994; Kemshall *et al.* 1997; Kemshall 1998a; Power 1994a, 1994b; Rose 1993). Consensus on the meaning and practice of risk is assumed, and implementation is seen as a matter of "common sense" (personal communication to the author by Home Office personnel), and management enforcement (Lawrie 1997; HMIP 1995, 1997). For researchers adopting this approach ethical issues remain unstated and obscured (Aubrey and Hough 1997; Roberts *et al.* 1996). Research is largely framed as policy-driven audits of current practice, and practice failings are seen as a matter for correction through the implementation of managerially desired assessment tools (Kemshall 1998a).

In this climate research which problematizes the notion of risk and adopts a constructivist epistemology to the investigation of risk practice is likely to encounter particular ethical and political difficulties. The British Sociological Association notes that when sociologists carry out research they "enter into personal and moral relationships with those they study" (1992: 704). However, the statement acknowledges that the discharge of ethical and moral responsibilities can be compromised "in situations of social conflict, competing social interests or where there is unanticipated misuse of the research by third parties" (1992: 704). This can be exacerbated in those situations where "disparities of power and status" exist (*ibid.*). These factors were particularly acute in the research discussed here. Whilst the original research was independently funded by the Economic and Social Research Council,[2] access to frontline probation staff was dependent upon management support, and the research subsequently attracted attention and further funding from the Home Office. This resulted in a significant change in the power relations within the initial research programme and presented a threat to the independence of the researcher.

Political issues arise most notably from the "forensic functions" of risk, that is, from the use of risk to attribute blame and allocate responsibility (Douglas 1986, 1992). For Douglas, the more culturally individualized a society becomes the more significant becomes the forensic potential of risk, literally a mechanism for holding individuals to account within a culture of diversity. Thus risk is central to the process of accountability and the allocation of responsibility in the light of things going wrong (Kemshall *et al.* 1997). Research into risk practices takes place within this politicization of risk, within which research knowledge may well be used to evaluate the competence of risk practitioners, to increase the accountability of workers, or to allocate blame away from the centre for subsequent risk failures. This can subject the researcher to severe pressure from central policy makers, particularly in those instances where research findings challenge the status quo (Grinyer 1995), critique the normative position of funders and policy makers, or fail to highlight the incompetence of workers. Research that fails to support the policy-driven intentions of central government policy makers is readily dismissed as "too academic" and contrary to the official position on risk.

This can leave the researcher working within what Grinyer (1995) has called "institutional bias", that is, within the official discourse on risk used by policy makers and managers. This "institutional bias" means that other constructions of risk are either ignored or delegitimated. The result is that only research within the official discourse of risk is commissioned or promoted by policy makers and central government funders. In these circumstances both frontline risk assessors and researchers can be disempowered.

The risk of challenge

Challenging and deconstructing the dominant official discourse of risk is not without risk. Researchers run the danger of placing themselves outside the "funding loop" or, at best, of having their work sidelined as being concerned with marginal sociological issues irrelevant to the world of policy implementation. This can be mirrored in difficulties with gatekeepers (Homan 1991), in this case senior service managers and policy makers, who will naturally seek to act in their own interests and seek to exercise power over both the conduct and dissemination of the research. Cohen and Taylor (1981) in their study of the Prison Service note how access can be the subject of prolonged negotiation, and research findings can be subjected to "anticipatory censorship" (1977: 79) in which expected findings are subtly discredited in advance of publication. Managing competing vested interest groups, often with differential power, is a challenge to the researcher. As Homan expresses it:

> Information is expensive and therefore not universally available, but it is often the basis of the retention of power, especially if its publication can be controlled. (1991: 176)

Unequal power relations are a feature of much contemporary social research. For Homan, this means that research participants give more than mere data:

> when they co-operate . . . they strengthen the position of those groups who control the flow of the information they collect. Social researchers must decide their own role in this process and may have misgivings about collecting data from individuals and delivering them to be . . . used by powerful institutions. (1991: 176)

Ethical research has been advocated as one strategy for reducing the impact of such effects upon the research process. However, what is meant by ethical research and how might it be applied in these circumstances?

The Notion of Ethical Research

The idea of ethical research is not particularly new, and its use has been advocated for the resolution of political conflicts and ethical dilemmas

Hazel Kemshall

(Gallagher *et al.* 1995). Within social work researchers have striven to emulate the accepted ethical principles of the profession (BASW 1988), and research in the psychological and sociological disciplines has been informed by similar principles (BSA 1992; BPS 1991).

Gallagher *et al.* (1995), drawing upon Beauchamp *et al.* (1982), have noted that such underlying principles are best summed up by notions of "autonomy, non-maleficence, beneficence and justice" (1995: 296), and that whilst often reflected in actual research procedures they are distinct underlying principles. For Gallagher *et al.* (1995) this distinction may in itself lead to difficulties as principles embedded in different procedures can conflict. As Kimmel (1988) has expressed it, situations can arise in which two desirable moral values conflict, and it is impossible to maximize both "simultaneously" (1988: 28). For example, beneficence and justice, particularly of the greater good, may only be achieved through the compromising of individual autonomy. Within social work and criminal justice practice this dilemma is commonly encountered by practitioners (for example, in contemporary probation practice the common good of victims is usually prioritized above the rights of offenders, particularly sex offenders). Such ethical dilemmas are resolved through concepts such as a "duty of care", and the pursuit of least harm and the most good, notions upheld in the courts when the competency of practice is tested (Carson 1996). However, in the reality of practice the resolution of dilemmas can be more variable, dependent upon the moral and professional values of the worker (Kemshall 1998a) and perceptions of role and responsibilities (Brearley 1982). This difficulty is reminiscent of Minichiello *et al.*'s distinction between "ethical absolutism" and "situational relativism" (1990: 233), with the former position claiming absolute and fixed underlying principles to guide all research, and the latter position highlighting the situational and contextual nature of ethical dilemmas which must therefore be resolved on a case-by-case basis.

Resolving ethical dilemmas

For researchers, the pursuit of ethical practice is no less complex (Adair *et al.* 1985). Whilst Beauchamp *et al.* (1982) identify key ethical principles, the procedures for their implementation in the research process can be variable. As Gallagher *et al.* (1995) illustrate, professional bodies produce statements of ethical principles but avoid statements of advice on the resolution of ethical conflicts (see, for example, the BSA statement, 1992: 703). This thorny issue is devolved to the researchers concerned.

Gallagher *et al.* outline three routine responses to ethical dilemmas: the *expedient*, the *value-driven*, and the *pragmatic* (1995: 300). The key component of the *expedient* approach is the designing out of ethical challenges from research methodologies, or the "off-loading" of ethical dilemmas to others such as ethics committees. Implicit in this response is a "value-neutral" approach to research, and a cultivated distance between researcher and researched. Ethical dilemmas are ultimately reduced to matters of technique and procedure. This response is closely paralleled by the *pragmatic* in which "tackling ethical dilemmas involves an assessment of the relative importance of each of the conflicting ethical principles" (Gallagher *et al.* 1995: 302). The response is dependent upon either ranking the relative importance of the ethical principles concerned, or of conducting a cost-benefit analysis. Essentially, both the expedient and pragmatic approaches reduce ethical dilemmas to matters of technique and cost-benefit calculations.

However, such analyses and ranking exercises are subject to the bias and values of the researcher(s) involved. Definitions of costs and indeed of benefits are subject to value framing (Kahneman and Tversky 1984) and cannot be expressed as value-neutral calculations (Adams 1995). Pragmatic resolutions may reflect implicit normative statements about the conduct of research, for example that research should meet the positivistic criteria of western science, or normative statements about what it is worthy to study, and which social problems deserve investigation and resolution. The key principle of cost-benefit analysis, for example, is the maximization of benefits and the minimization of costs (or harms) (Levine 1975). However, a large body of research into cost-benefit analyses of risk, for example across a range of activities as diverse as economics, social care, engineering, environmental risks, and the introduction of new technologies, demonstrates that such analyses are subject to value-framing and social constructions of legitimacy and acceptability (Douglas 1986). It is unlikely that researcher decisions on the relative harms to research participants of their research choices, or the benefits of conducting specific types of research will be immune to such dynamics. The pragmatic response largely hides such issues of value and there is a tendency to adopt the approach in a rather haphazard fashion (as described by Gallagher *et al.*, 1995, in their work). In some instances, of course, the actual cost-benefit equation will only be known after the event and with the benefit of hindsight. Research participants, for example, may express very different cost-benefit views to those of researchers once the outcome and application of the research is known.

Expediency also has risks. The researcher may become prey to various vested interests in an effort to gain consent, or to "get the research done". On-the-hoof compromises are likely as situations of conflict or challenge are decided so as to keep the research on track rather than from any explicit ethical position. Powerful vested interests are likely to exert disproportionate influence over the research process, particularly those who gate-keep funds or access, and sometimes at the expense of research participants.

The *value-driven* approach is openly directed by the values of the researcher and is acknowledged by the British Sociological Association "Statement of ethical practice" reference to the fact that

> it will be necessary to make such choices on the basis of principles and values, and the interests of those involved. (1992: 703)

For Gallagher *et al.* (1995) this is the weakest position on the grounds that it can be driven by self-interest, ends justifying means, and is highly variable in use depending upon the background and value-base of the researcher. For Gallagher *et al.* such self-interest and bias should be tempered by reference to colleagues and ethics committees. However, this assumes that such colleagues and committees are themselves free from bias and vested interest, and that issues of value are best resolved by recourse to the tactics of expediency. It also suggests that research can be a value-neutral exercise, a position queried by Weber over 60 years ago in his thesis on the sociology of knowledge (Weber 1936).

Action research: an ethical position?

Proponents of action research would take issue with Gallagher *et al.*'s view of the value-driven approach. Minichiello *et al.*, for example, describe action research as

> research in which the role and political stance of the researcher is aligned and interventionist. This is because research is joined with action in order to plan, implement and monitor change. Researchers choose to become participants in planned policy initiatives and use their knowledge and research expertise to aid their informants. (1990: 246)

In action research values are integral and explicitly stated. In recent years this has resulted in a growing body of research that reflects particular positions, including feminist research (Humphries 1999), research aimed at promoting equality and reducing poverty (Holman 1987), research with an explicit commitment to social justice (House 1991), and "participatory research approaches committed to empowerment" (Shaw 2000). This last has not been confined solely to the empowerment of service users, but has also encompassed a commitment to the development and empowerment of practitioners (Everitt and Hardiker 1996). Evaluative research in social care, for example, has witnessed a growing commitment to the twin aims of reflective practice and empowerment evaluation (Kemshall and Littlechild 2000; Shaw 2000).

Whilst such approaches are often successful in making the research stance of the researcher explicit and in highlighting the political dilemmas embedded in the research enterprise (Shaw 2000), they do not necessarily assist the researcher in escaping difficult ethical dilemmas. Differential power and social relations between researcher and researched have been noted as particularly problematic (Acker *et al.* 1983), and the difficulty in challenging existing power structures (Barnes and Wistow 1992) or balancing the competing interests of various users (Fisher 1992) have also been reviewed.

However, these developments have importantly focused upon the *process* of research as well as the use subsequently made of research output. The attention drawn to the political nature of the research enterprise has been particularly helpful (Weiss 1987) and these various examples of value-driven action research have made a significant contribution to the recognition of ethical and political issues as key components of research.

Practice Guidance for Ethical Research

Whilst Gallagher *et al.* (1995) present three distinct approaches to the resolution of ethical dilemmas and recount how they drew upon the pragmatic approach within their own work, these distinctions may be less evident in practice. Ethical absolutism may be an ideal difficult to adhere to in the *Realpolitik* of practice, and distinct approaches to problem resolution less easy to discern. However, it is possible and appropriate for researchers to outline clear principles and guiding parameters for their work. In the risk research reviewed here the following were adopted:

- *Commitment to the ethical code of conduct and principles of the profession under investigation*   This was informed by an early decision in the work that the researcher should respect the professional code of conduct of the workforce being researched and seek to avoid activities in the field that would be disruptive or undermining of such professional principles.
- *Commitment to the ethical code of conduct on confidentiality, access, dissemination etc. of the British Sociological Association (1992)*   During the preparation of the research proposal and the initial negotiation of research access the standards contained in this code were seen as the guiding parameters of the research profession, and therefore the standards against which both research proposals and research conduct would be judged by peers.
- *Reciprocity: the acknowledgement of participants' time and commitment, and strategies for "pay-back"*   Reciprocity was built into the original research proposal, and time and strategies for reciprocity were outlined including: quarterly feedback sessions with research participants, training sessions, and consultancy.
- *Mutuality in the conduct of the research and in the treatment of research participants*   This approach to the conduct of the research embodied respect and value for persons, and the recognition that research inquiry is a process of exchange and mutual learning.
- *Recognition of the researcher's role and responsibilities combined with rigorous self-monitoring*   This is crucial in those situations where the researcher may be co-opted by people in positions of power. Resistance to often subtle political processes and manipulation requires high levels of self-reflection and self-monitoring. In some circumstances an independent mentor may provide a useful service to the researcher.
- *Commitment to action research*   This was made explicit in the original proposal and during the negotiation of access. Individual participants were informed of the likely practice and policy implications of the research and how they would be informed of these developments. The quarterly feedback sessions were actively used to discuss results, dissemination issues, and practice/policy implications. The relevant professional journal was also extensively used. The final stage of the research process used a subsample of the original research participants to comment upon the results of the research through a series of group discussions and the use of critical path analysis (Kemshall 1998b). The latter enabled a degree of validation of research results from research participants.
- *Management of vested interests*   The difficulty of vested interests in the conduct of risk practice within the profession was recognized at the outset. The original research tender proposed a steering group comprising representatives of the various vested interest groups including central government policy makers, union personnel and research participants. This initially

worked well, and provided a venue for sharing ongoing research results and for initiating policy and practice discussions. However, during the course of the ESRC research, the researcher was commissioned by two of the interest groups to work on risk assessment. This compromised the independence of the researcher, and exposed the researcher to the subtle political processes outlined by Punch (1986). Both the rationale and usefulness of the steering group was undermined by the change of power relations as two vested interest groups in effect became funders and gatekeepers of research. Researchers cannot ignore the impact of vested interests in sensitive and contested areas, but this example illustrates the importance of clear parameters in their management, and clarity and consistency about the research role. If the researcher cannot manage this process with integrity, then other strategies will be required if the research is to maintain a degree of independence from political manipulation.

- *Acceptance and application of ethical relativism: the principle of the defensible decision*
This position recognizes that whilst basic principles and clear parameters can be outlined at the outset of the research process, the *Realpolitik* of fieldwork necessitates situationally specific "judgement calls". Competing choices must be resolved in situations of uncertainty and where all the future consequences of the decision cannot be known. Research choices, especially about risk research, are themselves a risky business. In this situation the adoption of the principle of the "defensible decision" from risk practice (Carson 1996; Kemshall 1996b, 1998a) may prove helpful. In essence, the principle recognizes that risk decisions are inherently uncertain, and that the full range of possible future outcomes arising from risk choices cannot be known. In these circumstances the correct course of action is only known through "hindsight" (Carson 1996) and practitioners are subject to retrospective bias in the evaluation of their judgements. Researchers are similarly exposed. In these circumstances defensibility has been seen as the key, that is, decisions have to be defensible in the light of hindsight bias. Central to judgements of defensibility is whether a body of peers would consider the decision to have been made in good faith, in line with current codes of practice and professional expectations, and at a level of competence recognized by the profession. Professional codes of conduct are therefore crucial, as is peer review and self-monitoring. Defensibility also requires public accounting and review of decisions combined with rigorous scrutiny by peers.

Conclusion

Whilst defensibility may seem to be a throwback to the expediency approach, it is not reducible to the pragmatic expediency of the researcher in the field. Hindsight scrutiny within accepted parameters is central and it provides a mechanism through which ethical decisions must be clearly articulated and justified. In a climate of increasing ethical relativism (Marshall and Rossman 1999) the defensible decision provides a useful benchmark for research practice in the field.

Notes

1. For a full review see Kemshall (1998a), ch. 4.
2. Risk in Probation Practice, sponsored by the Economic and Social Research Council's Risk and Human Behaviour programme, grant number L211252018.

References

Abu-Samah, A. (1996), Empowering research process: using groups in research to empower people, *Groupwork*, 9, 2: 221–52.

Acker, J., Barry, K., and Esseveld, J. (1983), Objectivity and truth: problems in doing feminist research, *Women's Studies International Forum*, 6, 4: 423–435.

Adair, J. G., Dushenko, T. W., and Lindsay, R. C. L. (1985), Ethical regulations and their impact on research practice, *American Psychologist*, 40, 1: 59–72.

Adams, J. (1995), *Risk*, London: University College Press.

Alaszewski, A., Harrison, L., and Manthorpe, G. (eds) (1998), *Risk, Health and Welfare*, Buckingham: Open University Press.

Aubrey, R., and Hough, M. (1997), *Assessing Offenders' Needs: Assessment Scales for the Probation Service*. A report for the Home Office Research and Statistics Directorate, London: Home Office.

Barnes, J. A. (1979), *Who Should Know What? Social Science, Privacy and Ethics*, Harmondsworth: Penguin.

Barnes, M., and Wistow, G. (1984), Involving carers in planning and review. In A. Connor and S. Black (eds), *Performance, Review and Quality in Social Care*, London: Jessica Kingsley.

Barnes, M., and Wistow, G. (eds) (1992), *Researching User Involvement*, Leeds: Nuffield Institute for Health Services Studies, University of Leeds.

Beauchamp, T. L., Faden, R. J., Wallace, R. J., and Walter, L. (1982), *Ethical Issues in Social Science Research*, Baltimore: Johns Hopkins University Press.

Beck, U. (1992), *Risk Society: Towards a New Modernity*, London: Sage.

Beck, U., Giddens, A., and Lash, S. (1994), *Reflexive Modernization*, Oxford: Polity Press in association with Blackwell.

Bloor, M. (1995a), A user's guide to contrasting theories of HIV-related risk behaviour. In J. Gabe (ed.), *Medicine, Health and Risk: Sociological Approaches*, Sociology of Health and Illness Monograph 1, Oxford: Blackwell, pp. 19–30.

Bloor, M. (1995b), *The Sociology of HIV Transmission*, London: Sage.

Bottoms, A. (1977), Reflections on the Renaissance of Dangerousness, *Howard Journal*, 16, 2: 70–96.

Brearley, C. P. (1982), *Risk in Social Work: Hazards and Helping*, London: Routledge and Kegan Paul.

British Association of Social Workers (BASW) (1988), *Code of Ethics for Social Work*, Birmingham: BASW.

British Psychological Society (BPS) (1991), *Code of Ethical Principles and Guidelines*, Leicester: British Psychological Society.

British Sociological Association (BSA) (1992), Statement of ethical practice, *Sociology*, 26, 4: 703–7.

Broadhead, R. S. (1982), Human rights and human subjects: ethics and strategies in social science research, *Sociological Inquiry*, 54: 107–23.

Carson, D. (1996), Risking legal repercussions. In H. Kemshall and J. Pritchard (eds), *Good Practice in Risk Assessment and Risk Management, vol. 1*, London: Jessica Kingsley.

Clarke, J., Cochrane, A., and McLaughlin, E. (eds) (1994), *Managing Social Policy*, London: Sage.

Hazel Kemshall

Cohen, S., and Taylor, L. (1981), *Psychological Survival*, 2nd edn, Harmondsworth: Penguin.
Douglas, M. (1986), *Risk Acceptability According to the Social Sciences*, London: Routledge and Kegan Paul.
Douglas, M. (1992), *Risk and Blame: Essays in Cultural Theory*, London: Routledge.
Everitt, A., and Hardiker, P. (1996), *Evaluating for Good Practice*, Basingstoke: Macmillan.
Everitt, A., and Hardiker, P. (1999), *Evaluating for Good Practice*, London: Macmillan Press.
Everitt, A., Hardiker, P., Littlewood, J., and Mullender, A. (1992), *Applied Research for Better Practice*, London: Macmillan.
Fisher, M. (1992), Users' experiences of agreements in social care. In M. Barnes and G. Wistow (eds), *Researching User Involvement*, Leeds: Nuffield Institute for Health Services Studies, University of Leeds.
Fleming, J., and Ward, D. (1999), Research as empowerment: the social action approach. In W. Shira and L. M. Wells (eds), *Empowerment Practice in Social Work: Developing Richer Conceptual Foundations*, Ontario, Canada: Canadian Scholar's Press.
Gallagher, B., Creighton, S., and Gibbons, J. (1995), Ethical dilemmas in social research: no easy solutions, *British Journal of Social Work*, 25: 295–311.
Giddens, A. (1990), *Consequences of Modernity*, Stanford, CA: Stanford University Press.
Giddens, A. (1991), *Modernity and Self Identify*, Oxford: Polity Press in association with Blackwell.
Grinyer, A. (1995), Risk, the real world and naïve sociology. In J. Gabe (ed.), *Medicine, Health and Risk: Sociological Approaches*, Sociology of Health and Illness Monograph 1, Oxford: Blackwell, pp. 31–51.
Grove-White, R. (1998), Risk society, politics and BSE. In J. Franklin (ed.), *The Politics of Risk Society*, Cambridge: Polity Press, pp. 50–3.
Her Majesty's Inspectorate of Probation (HMIP) (1995), *Dealing with Dangerous People: The Probation Service and Public Protection*, Report of a thematic inspection, London: Home Office.
Her Majesty's Inspectorate of Probation (HMIP) (1997), Risk management guidance. In Home Office/Association of Chief Officers of Probation, *The Management and Assessment of Risk*, London: Home Office/ACOP.
Holman, B. (1987), Research from the underside, *British Journal of Social Work*, 17, 6: 669–83.
Homan, R. (1991), *The Ethics of Social Research*, London: Longman.
Home Office (1997a), Risk/needs assessment. In Home Office/Association of Chief Officers of Probation, *The Management and Assessment of Risk*, London: Home Office/ACOP.
Home Office (1997b), *The Crime Sentences Act*, London: HMSO.
Home Office (1998), *The Crime and Disorder Act*, London: HMSO.
Home Office (1999), *The Offender Assessment System. Draft Risk Assessment Tool*, London: Home Office.
Home Office Circular 39 (1997), *The Sex Offender Act*, London: Home Office.
House, E. (1991), Evaluation and social justice: where are we now? In M. McLaughlin and D. Phillips (eds), *Evaluation and Education at Quarter Century*, Chicago: Chicago University Press.
Humphries, B. (1999), Feminist evaluation. In I. Shaw and J. Lishman (eds), *Evaluation and Social Work Practice*, London: Sage.
Irwin, A., and Wynne, B. (1996), *Misunderstanding Science? The Public Reconstruction of Science and Technology*, Cambridge: Cambridge University Press.
Kahneman, D., and Tversky, A. (1984), Choices, values, and frames, *American Psychologist*, 39, 4: 341–50.

Kemshall, H. (1996a), Offender risk and probation practice. In H. Kemshall and J. Pritchard (eds), *Good Practice in Risk Assessment and Management, vol. 1*, London: Jessica Kingsley.

Kemshall, H. (1996b), *Risk Workshops for Senior Managers*, London: Home Office Probation Training Unit/Association of Chief Probation Officers.

Kemshall, H. (1997), Sleep safely: crime risks may be smaller than you think, *Social Policy & Administration*, 31, 3: 247–59.

Kemshall, H. (1998a), *Risk in Probation Practice*, Aldershot: Ashgate.

Kemshall, H. (1998b), Enhancing risk decision making through critical path analysis, *Social Work Education*, 17, 4: 419–35.

Kemshall, H. (2000), *The Assessment and Management of Sexual and Violent Offenders*, London: Home Office, Policing and Reducing Crime Unit.

Kemshall, H., and Littlechild, R. (2000), *Researching for Participation and Involvement in Social Care*, London: Jessica Kingsley.

Kemshall, H., Parton, N., Walsh, M., and Waterson, J. (1997), Concepts of risk in relation to organizational structure and functioning within the personal social services and probation, *Social Policy & Administration*, 31, 3: 213–32.

Kemshall, H., and Pritchard, J. (eds) (1996), *Good Practice in Risk Assessment and Risk Management, vol. 1*, London: Jessica Kingsley.

Kemshall, H., and Pritchard, J. (eds) (1997), *Good Practice in Risk Assessment and Risk Management: Protection, Rights and Responsibilities, vol. 2*, London: Jessica Kingsley.

Kimmel, A. J. (ed.) (1988), *Ethics and Values in Applied Social Research*, Newbury Park, CA: Sage.

Lawrie, C. (1997), Risk: the role and responsibilities of middle managers. In H. Kemshall and J. Pritchard (eds), *Good Practice in Risk Assessment and Management: Protection, Rights and Responsibilities, vol. 2*, London: Jessica Kingsley, pp. 301–11.

Levine, R. J. (1975), The role of assessment of risk-benefit criteria in the determination of the appropriateness of research involving human subjects. In *National Commission for the Protection of Biomedical and Behavioural Research, Appendix, volume 1: The Belmont Report*, Bethesda, MD: Department of Health, Education and Welfare.

Lupton, D. (1999), *Risk*, London: Routledge.

Marshall, C., and Rossman, G. B. (1999), *Designing Qualitative Research*, 3rd edn, London: Sage.

Minichiello, V., Aroni, R., Timewell, E., and Alexander, L. (1990), *In-depth Interviewing: Researching People*, Cheshire: Longman.

Petersen, A. R. (1996), Risk and the regulated self: the discourse of health promotion as politics of uncertainty, *Australian and New Zealand Journal of Sociology*, 32, 1: 44–57.

Power, M. (1994a), *The Audit Explosion*, London: Demos.

Power, M. (1994b), The audit society. In A. G. Hopwood and P. Miller (eds), *Accounting as Social and Institutional Practice*, Cambridge: Cambridge University Press.

Punch, M. (1986), *The Politics and Ethics of Fieldwork*, Qualitative Research Methods Series 3, London: Sage.

Reason, P. (ed.) (1980), *Human Inquiry in Action: Developments in New Paradigm Research*, London: Routledge and Kegan Paul.

Roberts, C., Burnett, R., Kirby, A., and Hamill, H. (1996), *A System for Evaluating Practice: Report of Method Devised and Piloted by the Oxford Probation Studies Unit and Warwickshire*, Oxford: Centre for Criminological Research.

Rose, N. (1993), Government, authority and expertise in advanced liberalism, *Economy and Society*, 22: 283–99.

Shaw, R. (2000), Just inquiry? Research and evaluation for service users. In H. Kemshall and R. Littlechild (eds), *Researching for Participation and Involvement in Social Care*, London: Jessica Kingsley.

Hazel Kemshall

Sieber, J. E., and Stanley, B. (1988), Ethical and professional dimensions of socially sensitive research, *American Psychologist*, 43, 1: 49–55.

Weber, M. (1936), *Ideology and Utopia*, London: Routledge and Kegan Paul.

Weiss, C. (1987), Where politics and evaluation meet. In D. Palumbo (ed.), *The Politics of Program Evaluation*, Newbury Park, CA: Sage.

Wynne, B. (1982), *Rationality and Ritual: The Windscale Inquiry and Nuclear Decisions in Britain*, London: British Society for the History of Science, 168.

Wynne, B. (1989), Sheep farming after Chernobyl, *Environment*, 31, 11–15: 33–9.

Wynne, B. (1996), May the sheep safely graze? A reflexive view of the expert–lay knowledge divide. In S. Lash, B. Szerszynski and B. Wynne (eds), *Risk, Environment and Modernity*, London: Sage, pp. 44–83.

9

Synthesizing Research and Practice: Using the Action Research Approach in Health Care Settings

Paul Bate

Keywords

Action research; Health care; Organization development; Cultural change

An Autobiographical Note and an Introduction

Most of my professional life has been spent working on major change projects in both public and private sector organizations—radical, large-scale trans-formations mainly of a "second order" or re-orientational nature (Bate 1995; Flamholtz and Randle 1998; Miles 1997; Taffinder 1998). In recent times this work has focused on hospital and health care organizations within the NHS, taking in some of the big issues around the current government's moderniza-tion agenda, such as re-engineering and patient process redesign, clinical and corporate governance, and structural and cultural change.

This has culminated in the present position I occupy, which is a joint chair shared between my university and a large urban teaching hospital, where I seek to combine the "outsider" role of academic researcher with the "in-sider" role of interventionist and professional helper (a parallel role to, say, a professor of medicine). The role involves giving intellectual input into the thinking processes of clinicians and managers, and helping them to bring about change: in their cultures, structures and processes. The position is a difficult and challenging one, though according to at least one observer in my discipline, well worth the effort. In a recent article in *Anthropology News*, Michael Oldani (1999) argues that this kind of integration of the sometimes conflicting roles of outsider and insider in corporations needs to come top of anthropology's agenda for the twenty-first century. Anthropologists, he states, need to come in from the outside, but must at the same time be able to maintain their independence and not allow their work to be censored or screened in any way (as is sometimes the case). I would interpret this as a challenge for us to find ways of *collaborating* but not *colluding* with the organ-izations we encounter, and the line between these can be very fine. My role offers one such model and way forward in this regard.

However, my paper is not specifically about that role, which is unique, but the approach and methods I have developed over time in order to be able to play it effectively. It is about anthropologists and social science researchers in general having an impact on action, and making a difference to those whose lives they observe and write about.

The hospital itself, whilst enjoying a national reputation for the high-quality care it provides, sits in a very depressed area of the city, with a large immigrant population and high levels of urban poverty and deprivation. The decision to commit valuable resources to creating a chair in management development resulted from a growing sense of unease within the hospital that it might be losing some of its "edge", that unless it began to embark upon a major programme of change it might end up as yet another example of "a successful organization that failed". Whilst its structures, cultures and practices had been perfectly in step with the "internal market" ideology of the Thatcher era, people recognized that this was no longer the case with the current Labour government's "partnership" emphasis that had replaced it.

The organization prided itself on its ability to "read the tea leaves" (as they put it) and to see national and local issues early, and had come to the view that a repositioning or realignment with the new context was needed if it was to retain its "star status". In particular its "battle-hardened structure" was tired and worn down (as were many of the incumbents) and needed to go through "a process of renewal" to make it more nimble and responsive. "Hero or zero?" was the blunt way one senior clinician put it, echoing the view of many that the organization had reached a critical point in its development, a kind of fork in the road, from where it could go either up or down. The intention was to launch the organization on a new growth curve, and my role would be (in their words) to provide the "intellectual soul" of their change effort.

What I have been doing is more than "applied" anthropology—more like "action anthropology" or "action ethnography". This term describes a situation where anthropological data and concepts are fed back to the parties involved to help them bring about change, thereby impacting directly on action. It is not a case of applying "my" framework: the aim is to develop a kind of ethnographic consciousness amongst the actors themselves (Bate 1997; Linstead 1997), so that they become lay ethnographers of their own practices.

My paper is therefore about doing OD (organization development) from an anthropological or cultural perspective, with the anthropologist as helper, coach and change agent. Specifically, it is about using ethnographic data for problem-solving, issue diagnosis and action-taking, and is therefore not just applied but action-based anthropology. It is about representing issues anthropologically, and getting people to "think culturally" about those issues (Bate 1997). In this regard it is also a re-framing device designed to help them step outside the box of their "normal" thinking. This is important if one is to bring about change, especially cultural change. As Marcel Proust so wonderfully put it:

> The real voyage of discovery begins not with visiting new places but in seeing familiar landscapes with new eyes.

In my experience, the cultural perspective helps the parties to do just this—in the words of the popular phrase, to "make the familiar strange".

Those who have attempted to combine the role of scholar and professional helper will know how difficult this can be. The best way I have found is to base it on the classic "action research" approach to organizational studies, which I have greatly modified over the years, incorporating my own discipline within it. The concept of action research was originally formulated by John Collier, US Commissioner of Indian Affairs in the 1940s. It was later developed for organizations by Kurt Lewin and his students J. R. P. French, Lester Coch, and Edgar Schein at Michigan University during the 1950s and 1960s (to become the foundation stone of the new discipline of OD), and finally by the Tavistock Institute in the 1970s and beyond (Bruce and Wyman 1998; Burke 1994).

The model went out of fashion for a time during the early 1980s but has since been enjoying something of a revival (Goldstein 1992; Hollingsworth 1997; Shani and Pasmore 1985; Zuber-Skerritt 1996). The reasons are two-fold: first, because of the huge growth of interest in OD and change management in recent years, from which action research has always been inseparable, and second, because of the new applications it has found in relation to today's highly fashionable concept of the "learning" or "knowledge-creating" organization (Senge 1990; Senge *et al.* 1999; Nonaka and Takeuchi 1995; Quinn 1992). While these latter writings are strong on the substantive aspects, what action research has brought are valuable insights into *how* a learning organization might be created. It has therefore become of particular interest to management trainers and consultants working with learning organization concepts "on the ground" (cf. Pedler *et al.* 1997).

At about the same time action research received a further boost from writers on research methods, who began to champion it as a form of inquiry which underscored the "new values" in contemporary research, such as relevance, utility, applicability and speed (Kemmis and McTaggart 1988; Stringer 1996). Others pointed to its humanistic qualities as a research method, the fact that it was collaborative, that research was done "with" people not "to" them (Reason 1994).

The action research model is certainly no stranger to health care organizations in either the UK or elsewhere (Boss 1989; Golembiewski 1987; Hart and Bond 1995; Margulies and Dundon 1987). A recent study by Morrison and Lilford (1999) showed it had gained ground in several branches of the UK health services, principally in health promotion, in nursing, and to a lesser extent in general practice and in the work of commissioning health authorities. One of the reasons has been pressure from the NHS Executive for greater speed in the gathering and utilization of data, especially patient and community data. Action research, with its simultaneous combining of data gathering, feedback and action, is an example of the kind of "rapid appraisal technique" the government and Executive have been pressing for within the NHS (Bowling 1998).

It has received an additional boost from the recent adoption of the principle of "evidence-based" practice, which insists that all available research knowledge be incorporated into the protocols of everyday practice. To put it the other way round, any clinical action, such as prescribing a particular drug, must always be based on "best evidence". This simple principle has put research and data in a much more prominent position, where they not only continue to provide the traditional "proof" for theory, but have now become a "proof" for practice as well.

The extension of the evidence-based principle into the field of management and organizational practice has not been long in coming, and it is here where the action research model is likely to be a major beneficiary in future years. The reason lies in the title, "action research"—actually a reversal of the real sequence, which is to conduct the research first and then to take the action, and in the light of the learning from this to undertake further research. Clearly this is the evidence-based approach under a different heading, the bringing together or synthesis of knowledge and practice. More than this, action research is not just an evidence-based methodology; it is in my view one of the few examples of an actual process for implementing an evidence-based approach.

But what of the relevance of this to anthropology, particularly organizational anthropology and those who practise it? In many ways the issues and concerns of current anthropology—and arguably the social sciences in general—are identical to those above. The search is clearly on, and has been for some time, to find more satisfactory ways of synthesizing theory and practice, the most recent bulletin of the National Association of Practising Anthropologists (NAPA) being a clear and most welcome example of this (Hill and Baba 1999, *The Unity of Theory and Practice in Anthropology: Rebuilding a Fractured Synthesis*). The theme is hardly new: NAPA has been treating it as a major issue for more than a decade and a half (cf. Baba 1986; Jordan 1994).

However, it is interesting that the action research model has not appeared anywhere in the picture so far. Either people have tended to write about the "consulting model" of anthropology (Baba 1986), which suggests an incidental or secondary role for the research element, or they have written about the "applied anthropology model", which reverses the emphasis and makes practice incidental or secondary to the research. Action research, as I conceive of it, lies somewhere in the adumbrated zone between the two, not one or the other but both. The strategic positioning of action research here points to research and practice being in some kind of balance (in fact a dynamic tension), such that over a period of time *researching* and *practising* become progressively symbiotic and interpenetrated within a single unified process— two sides of the same coin. Traditional demarcation lines are broken. One stops thinking (and talking) of "theorists" or "practitioners", since they have become blurred and indistinguishable; all one sees, or should see if everything is working properly, are "theorizing practitioners" and "practising theorists". There is a fusion of research and practice within both roles.

Action research is therefore neither consulting nor applied research (nor is it a hybrid: its paradigm and methods are quite different). The hospital knew this too, having rejected consulting on the grounds of its being "too expensive, too externally driven, and too short-term" and applied research by the local university as "too academic and too lacking in practical emphasis and action outcomes".

The Model in Close-up

No action without research, and no research without action. (Kurt Lewin)

For those not familiar with the action research approach, my version of it, which has evolved from my repeated experiences of using it, can be seen in figure 1.[1]

Let us examine the model in more detail. In the *diagnostic phase* the focus of investigation is the "what" question. What are the issues, what are the current problems and challenges as people see them? What in their view does the organization need to start doing, stop doing, do less of, or do more of? These questions tend to touch on very basic, down-to-earth kinds of things like the sadness and anger about the decline of the hospital, or the lack of honest communication, or the shortcomings of the top management team. Though well known and widely discussed by all—after all, they are their issues and their words—these take on extra power and significance when at the *feedback* stage they are "spoken by an actor", on a public rather than private stage, up-front rather than behind the hand, yet still their words. Hence my earlier comment about making the familiar strange. A lot of issues in organizations are "known but not said", and certainly not shared.

It would be quite wrong to see the feedback and discussion phase as being purely about clarification and definition. It is really about getting people to confront and "own" their problems, and to this extent it is not just a description and illustration of the issues but an invitation for them to become more "reflective practitioners" and, even more than that, to develop a radical critique of their customary ways of working. Although there is a natural tendency in such a process to focus on the "negative aspects" (most analysis is problem-centred), the aim should be to construct a balanced picture of the whole scene, good and bad, what Koster and Bouman (1999) refer to appropriately as "the balanced change card".

The issue is not just one of content: style of engagement is equally important. The rules are not to be cruel or to put people too much on the defensive by singling out individuals. Action feedback calls for "compassionate confrontation" and acts of kindness, though not a ducking of the issues. One of the strengths of the culture perspective is that it puts the emphasis upon the *folies-à-deux* and *collective* stupidities which people create, thus conveniently de-individualizing problems and stressing the shared responsibility for these. Hence it is not a case of *mea culpa* but of *all of us* accepting some part of the blame.

Imagine the following quotations being read out in an action research setting, particularly the third set of examples, where the top team members were actually present to hear what people had been saying about them—although all references to named individuals were removed. The examples are all taken from a previous action research project, involving a very different organization from the present one. This was an organization in crisis, one that had lost its "steering capacity", and was described ironically by one staff member as a "sick organization treating sick patients".

Paul Bate

Figure 1

Implementing change: the "action research" approach

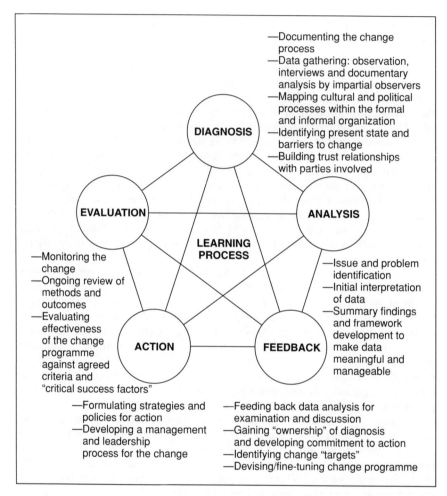

—Documenting the change process
—Data gathering: observation, interviews and documentary analysis by impartial observers
—Mapping cultural and political processes within the formal and informal organization
—Identifying present state and barriers to change
—Building trust relationships with parties involved

DIAGNOSIS

EVALUATION

ANALYSIS

LEARNING PROCESS

—Monitoring the change
—Ongoing review of methods and outcomes
—Evaluating effectiveness of the change programme against agreed criteria and "critical success factors"

—Issue and problem identification
—Initial interpretation of data
—Summary findings and framework development to make data meaningful and manageable

ACTION

FEEDBACK

—Formulating strategies and policies for action
—Developing a management and leadership process for the change

—Feeding back data analysis for examination and discussion
—Gaining "ownership" of diagnosis and developing commitment to action
—Identifying change "targets"
—Devising/fine-tuning change programme

Issue 1: Organization decline/growing pessimism of outlook

"Up until five years ago this was a hospital of which I could be proud, and when people criticized it at dinner parties I would say to my colleagues 'that's not very good, is it?' But now, if someone says it's crap, I say 'Yes that's right.' That's a sadness but that's the situation." (Clinical consultant)

"Three years ago things in the hospital were very upbeat and optimistic. The sky was the limit. Since then things have clearly gone downhill. There is a common perception

that we have lost our way. It is currently unclear as to where it is we are trying to get." (Anaesthetist)

"So here we are eleven years on and still no change. No wonder there's so much cynicism and disillusionment. People are saying, 'well if I stand still, they will all run round in circles and they'll be back shortly.' There is a lot in that. Certainly, it is less and less easy to give credibility to people who come with yet another bright scheme, and be able to say, 'Oh yes, tell me about it.'" (Senior nurse)

Issue 2: Propaganda and "spin"/the culture of secrets

"I was standing on a balcony with a colleague saying, 'Shall we jump?' and she just laughed and said, 'If we do, you know all we'll get is a centre-spread from the communications department saying, "Loyal staff jump to their death in bid to save hospital"'... I think people want some honesty, instead of everything positive all the time when it is not. Let's be honest, you know, and work together. We could if people knew where they stood." (Nurse)

Issue 3: Top management team

Indecisive:

"There is complete exasperation—will somebody please make a decision and let us get on with doing something. Even if we have to change because we've made the wrong decision, at least let's make a decision. But they don't seem to. I don't know what the Board do, but this is the perception of the organization. The joke, if you want to know, is that they're frightened rabbits." (Surgeon)

Distant and removed:

"A lovely nurse who is lost to this organization now and one of the few people I'd really like to go and take George [senior manager] *by the throat about said 'When I first came to this organization I was told that the senior management had an open door policy. What a bloody shame they never came out of it.'"* (Senior nurse)

Uncomfortable with emotional issues:

"My own staff appraisal is a good example. I had been led to believe I was going to be upgraded, and she [senior manager] *said quite coldly 'No, not this time around. Sorry.' Well I just burst into tears, and all she did was to turn round and tell me that she could* never *cry to her boss."* (Nurse adviser)

Avoidance of conflict:

"If you try to raise issues with them that are difficult, if you try to address conflict, you find you are cut out completely." (Business manager)

Paul Bate

Lack of strategic direction:

"Where are the strategic goals and how are we going to get there? This is lacking throughout this whole organization. The result is the nonsense we have just had where we appoint a new vascular surgeon when there are no plans to increase vascular work." (Physician)

In many ways this is all fairly standard OD (defining the issues, articulating the "felt need" and developing a compelling case for change) but the difference occurs at the *analytical/interpretative stage* of the model where the "what" begins to give way to the "why" question: why do these problems exist and why do they *persist?*—when participants are encouraged to "think culturally" about their problems and to try putting a different frame around them. In this situation, anthropology is being used as a method and a paradigm of explanation and interpretation. Through it one is suggesting that problems may have a root in the "culture" of the organization, which in an action sense suggests that cultural change, not just change at a structural or behavioural level, may be what is actually required.

Building on what they themselves had told me I suggested to staff that many of their problems could be traced back, root and branch, to a cultural source (though ultimately it would be for them to decide whether the case had been made: the challenge of action research is feeding back and opening up one's analysis to those involved and letting them judge). In fact there seemed to be three main roots, what they themselves subsequently labelled the "culture of tribalism" (linked to problems of co-ordination), the "culture of individualism" (problems of accountability), and the "culture of conservatism" (problems of innovation and change). Each of these "isms" (and there were many sub-branches) drew attention to a dysfunctional mindset within the organization, a form of "schematic myopia" (Harris 1990) or a "vicious circle of thinking" (Masuch 1985) which conspired to perpetuate or escalate the problems. The "ism" suffix denoted an excess of something, a state of mind over which the victims had lost control:

> They are somehow trapped in the web of their own actions. The hidden score is their own, but they don't like the music. Unable to stop, they play the unpleasant tune over and over again. (Masuch 1985: 15)

As with the diagnosis, the analysis itself was again a collage of the staff's own words and comments. The difference was that these were now transposed into a new frame and given different labels. This is how those involved—not just the top management but a wide range of stakeholders throughout the organization—came to embark on a new journey, one which in this case led them to a reconstruction of their problems (and ultimately their solutions) in cultural terms. The three cultural issues are illustrated by the three "isms" listed in the boxes.

Part of the process of feeding back may involve presenting ethnographic material in a visual way through pictures or cartoons, images for world-building that reduce complex issues to manageable sizes, which at the same

---

"Ism" 1

The culture of tribalism (problems of lateral coordination
between professional groups)

"We are a tribal organization. We think of ourselves as antagonists and rivals. Tribal relations are there, they're real, they're insidious. I don't know how we are ever going to find a consensus on the best way to move forward. It's all about factions. It's all about turf battles and the politics around people's patch or their territory." (Middle manager)

"Here is a clear example of two tribes who don't hold each other in high esteem, and who, through their troubled relations have set the whole tone for the hospital. Somewhere the tribalism has to come into the solution. It has to be taken as an issue and worked on. This would give a lead to the rest of the organization, so that other groups begin to follow suit." (Senior manager)

"Ism" 2

The culture of individualism (problems of accountability)

"I went on this management course and the tutor put up this diagram, which had all the nicely structured management systems for nurses, porters and technicians. And in the middle was this cloud which were the consultants, and he said, 'This first lot correspond to the normal structure of management, and you can change it or modify it according to what's going on in the environment. But this bunch, the consultants, float about and when something impinges on their area they just fire off letters or fax the chairman. And there's no way of controlling what they are up to.'" (Medical consultant)

"There is no accountability structure for consultants. They are not regulated. They go over budget; sometimes that is necessary, sometimes not. They ignore directives they don't like. They fight amongst each other but if they feel threatened they band together as a powerful force. How do you manage in that situation?" (Operations manager)

"Ism" 3

The culture of conservatism (problems of innovation and change)

"We don't have change here. We're a completely floating nebulous wobble of an organization." (Manager)

"Changing the culture? Here? It's like trying to kill a dinosaur. You know, you can shoot it in its tiny brain, but the legs keep thrashing for a very long time afterwards." (Trust board member)

"I expect many people look on us as a 1970s trade union, exercising our block vote. There are the same demarcation and jurisdictional issues as a trade union. We also jealously guard our jobs and areas; good old-fashioned protectionism." (Anaesthetist)

---

time help to defrost what is often a difficult process. Cartoons are idealized and simplified models which offer the added bonus of allowing people to laugh at themselves and each other, and generally not to take themselves *too* seriously. Self-parody is very important to the change process, and cartoons such as those reproduced here help defuse what might otherwise be angry destructive encounters, while at the same time getting people to face up to their problem mentalities—in this case the "tribalism" that threatens to sink the boat or isolate people on their separate islands (see pp. 488, 489). People instantly recognized themselves and their organization in the cartoon, albeit as a caricature of real life.

Inviting participants to create their own isms can be an important part of the action research project. Certainly people seem to find it much easier to engage with the ism than the more troubling concept of "culture", and it does seem to be a useful linguistic device for identifying dominant, yet hitherto elusive, "bad habits of thinking" within an organization.

Most organization development is about getting the present and future clear, the maxim being:

If you want to find out where you want to be, begin by finding out where you are.

Normally the "present state—desired state" analysis is a fairly unremarkable technique for finding out where you are, where you want to be, and how you are going to get there (Beckhard 1997; Beckhard and Harris 1977; Beckhard and Pritchard 1992). However, when used in a more anthropological way, especially in the later analytical phases of the process, it becomes more of a heuristic—an aid to thinking—than a method, its purpose being to get the participants to model the required cultural shifts "in the round" as part of a total system view of their organizational situation. One such attempt is shown in figure 2 and a more sophisticated one from another organization in figure 3.

The charts themselves—a few seemingly random signifiers—might at first glance seem an unlikely basis on which to develop a strategy for change in a complex organization. But implicitly they contained powerful messages about the need to move towards a flatter, more flexible and adaptive culture, less controlling and more collaborative, one which valued partnership and diversity.

There were two main reasons why these charts were such powerful pieces of paper, and why they subsumed all the mission statements, reports, stakeholder maps and organizational analyses which accompanied them. First they contained a public record, for everyone to see, of the vocabulary in which people were framing their expectations and aspirations for change. Because the charts had been developed through an inclusive consultation process, they became symbols of common ownership, carrying an implicit message that the spirit of collaboration would persist as the programmes gathered pace. A wide constituency of support could thus be developed, helping bring the necessary sponsorship, commitment and time to the programmes.

Second, the charts provided a sort of "ethic" for the terms on which the change would occur. As a senior nurse pointed out to us: *"I've got that from/to pinned to my desk and it makes me think about what I'm doing and say 'Hold on, is this what we want from the new culture?'—and it seems to touch on my staff and other departments I come into contact with as well. I mean no-one can deny it's the change we need—we all said it."*

This "ethic" proved particularly powerful at the *evaluation* stage of the action research process, when people began to look back and take stock of how far they had travelled and how successful they had been. Evaluation is clearly about details—reviews of action taken and so forth—but it is also about whether the spirit of the endeavour has been realized or sustained: this, too, is important in a change process. People need to ask themselves whether their actions have been consistent with the organization they have been attempting to create. The "from-to" chart, in this sense, evoked a wider organizational conscience: this is what we all agreed to, this is the organization we felt we needed, and this is the culture we wanted to create. So did we do it?

A Final Word

This paper has suggested that there may be a middle way between research and consultancy in the form of the action research model, which offers a method of research and intervention and also a process for change. The aim of the schematic presented in this paper is to suggest how a change project might move from data gathering and analysis to feedback and discussion, to

framework building, action and evaluation, and on to further research. Given the opportunistic, exploratory and emergent nature of most action research, these activities will not necessarily follow in strict order, hence the multiple lines of connection in figure 1 above. It thus draws attention to the limits of planning and prediction in change processes, and emphasizes that change is not imposed, or even knowable, but discovered as it happens as part of an ongoing learning process.

This learning is not only about action but also about representing the organization in novel and different ways: dressing the familiar landscape in

Figure 2

Cultural change

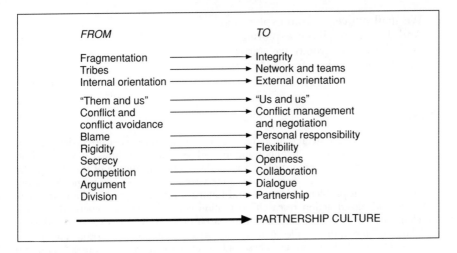

FROM		TO
Fragmentation	⟶	Integrity
Tribes	⟶	Network and teams
Internal orientation	⟶	External orientation
"Them and us"	⟶	"Us and us"
Conflict and conflict avoidance	⟶	Conflict management and negotiation
Blame	⟶	Personal responsibility
Rigidity	⟶	Flexibility
Secrecy	⟶	Openness
Competition	⟶	Collaboration
Argument	⟶	Dialogue
Division	⟶	Partnership

⟶ PARTNERSHIP CULTURE

Figure 3

Organization culture and ethos

Dimensions

1. Power

Control	. . .	Collaboration
Compliance	. . .	Commitment
Darwinism	. . .	Mutual support
Fear/punishment	. . .	Recognition/reward

2. Work

Task-centred	. . .	People-centred
Action focus	. . .	Learning/reflection
Fail-safe/low-risk	. . .	Safe to fail
Fads and fashions	. . .	Selective innovation
Planning	. . .	Opportunism

3. Internal and external relationships

Tribalism	. . .	Networks/partnerships
Conflict avoidance	. . .	Conflict management/negotiation
Culture of blame	. . .	Collective responsibility
Culture of secrets	. . .	Openness
Adversarialism	. . .	Alliances
Insular	. . .	Cosmopolitan

Paul Bate

different colours. The result is a more intense sense of the present, what the playwright Denis Potter once described as the "nowness of the now". People begin to see things anew, as if for the first time:

> We shall not cease from exploration
> And the end of all our exploring
> Will be to arrive where we started
> And know the place for the first time.

(T. S. Eliot, Four Quartets)

Note

1. I have deliberately steered away from giving an abstract generalized definition of the term "action research", choosing instead to focus upon how I have used it in my own practice. There is in fact a wide divergence in the use of the term in the literature, and it would therefore be quite wrong to suggest any single definition. Accepting this problem, Morrison and Lilford (1999) have proposed an extremely useful "idealized action research" definition consisting of five tenets which they claim may be found in most action research projects. These are: (1) the "flexible planning" tenet, the detailed content and direction of a research project are not to be determined at the outset. These only take shape as the work progresses, and are kept continuously under review; (2) the "iterative cycle" tenet, research activity proceeds by a cycle of defining the problem, proposing action, taking action, learning the lessons of that action, and reconsidering the problem in the light of those lessons, and so on; (3) the "subjective meaning" tenet, the subjective meanings which those involved attach to the problem must be allowed to determine the content, direction and measures of success of a research project; (4) the "simultaneous improvement" tenet, a research project must set out to change the problem situation for the better in the very process of researching it; (5) the "unique context" tenet, the project must take into account the unique nature of the social context in which the project is carried out. Certainly all five of these apply to my own research, and in my view excellently capture the essence and the common denominators of action research.

References

Baba, M. L. (ed.) (1986), *Business and Industrial Anthropology: an Overview*, NAPA Bulletin, 2, American Anthropological Association.

Bate, S. P. (1995), *Strategies for Cultural Change*, 2nd reprint, Oxford: Butterworth Heinemann.

Bate, S. P. (1997), Whatever happened to organizational anthropology? A review of the field of organizational ethnography and anthropological studies, *Human Relations*, 50, 9: 1147–75.

Beckhard, R. (1997), *Agent of Change: My Life, My Practice*, San Francisco: Jossey-Bass.

Beckhard, R., and Harris, R. (1977), *Organizational Transitions: Managing Complex Change*, Reading, MA: Addison-Wesley.

Beckhard, R., and Pritchard, W. (1992), *Changing the Essence: the Art of Creating and Leading Fundamental Change in Organizations*, San Francisco: Jossey-Bass.

Boss, R. W. (1989), *Organization Development in Health Care*, Reading, MA: Addison-Wesley.

Bowling, A. (1998), *Research Methods in Health: Investigating Health and Health Services*, Buckingham: Open University Press.

Bruce, R., and Wyman, S. (1998), *Changing Organizations: Practicing Action Training and Research*, Thousand Oaks, CA: Sage.

Burke, W. W. (1994), *Organization Development: a Process of Learning and Changing*, Reading, MA: Addison-Wesley.

Flamholtz, E. G., and Randle, Y. (1998), *Changing the Game: Organizational Transformations of the First, Second, and Third Kinds*, New York: Oxford University Press.

Goldstein, J. (1992), Beyond planning and prediction: bringing back action research to O. D., *Organisation Development Journal*, 10, 2: 1–7.

Golembiewski, R. T. (1987), Diagnosis for health care providers and their systems: an entry design and its supporting theory, *Consultation: An International Journal*, 6, 4: 265–80.

Harris, S. G. (1990), A schema-based perspective on organization culture. Paper presented to the *Annual Meeting of the American Academy of Management*, Washington DC, August.

Hart, E., and Bond, M. (1995), *Action Research for Health and Social Care: a Guide to Practice*, Buckingham: Open University Press.

Hill, C. E., and Baba, M. L. (eds) (1999), *The Unity of Theory and Practice in Anthropology: Rebuilding a Fractured Synthesis*, NAPA Bulletin 18, American Anthropology Association.

Hollingsworth, S. (1997), *International Action Research: a Casebook for Educational Reform*, Brighton: Falmer Press. (See especially A. Tichen, Creating a learning culture: a story of change in hospital nursing.)

Jordan, A. T. (ed.) (1994), *Practicing Anthropology in Corporate America: Consulting on Organisational Culture*, NAPA Bulletin 14, American Anthropological Association.

Kemmis, S., and McTaggart, P. (1988), *The Action Research Planner*, Deakin University.

Koster, E., and Bouman, W. (1999), The balanced *change* card: a framework for designing and assessing organisational change processes. Paper presented to the *Annual Meeting of the American Academy of Management*, Chicago, August.

Linstead, S. (1997), The social anthropology of management, *British Journal of Management*, 8: 85–98.

Margulies, N., and Dundon, M. W. (1987), Organization development and health organizations, *Consultation: An International Journal*, 6, 3: 221–35.

Masuch, M. (1985), Vicious circles in organizations, *Administrative Science Quarterly*, 30: 14–33.

Miles, R. H. (1997), *Leading Corporate Transformation*, Jossey-Bass: San Francisco.

Morrison, B., and Lilford, R. (1999), Action research and health services: applicability in theory. Unpublished manuscript, University of Birmingham, Department of Public Health and Epidemiology, School of Medicine.

Nonaka, I., and Takeuchi, H. (1995), *The Knowledge-creating Company*, New York: Oxford University Press.

Oldani, M. J. (1999), Profit makers vs. profit takers, *Anthropology News*, 40, 8, November: 7–8.

Pedler, M., Burgoyne, J., and Boydell, T. (1997), *The Learning Company: a Strategy for Sustainable Development*, 2nd edn, New York: McGraw-Hill.

Quinn, J. B. (1992), *Intelligent Enterprise: a Knowledge and Service Based Paradigm for Industry*, New York: Free Press.

Reason, P. (1994), Three approaches to participative inquiry. In N. K. Denzin and Y. S. Lincoln (eds), *Handbook of Qualitative Research*, Thousand Oaks, CA: Sage.

Senge, P. (1990), *The Fifth Discipline: the Art and Practice of the Learning Organization*, New York: Doubleday.

Senge, P., Roberts, C., Ross, R., Smith, B., Roth, G., and Kleiner, A. (1999), *The Dance of Change: the Challenges of Sustaining Momentum in Learning Organisations*, London: Nicholas Brealey.

Paul Bate

Shani, A. B., and Pasmore, W. A. (1985), Organizational inquiry: towards a new model of the action research process. In D. D. Warwick (ed.), *Contemporary Organization Development: Current Thinking and Applications*, Glenview, IL: Scott Foreman.

Stringer, E. T. (1996), *Action Research: a Handbook for Practitioners*, London: Sage.

Taffinder, P. (1998), *Big Change: a Route-map for Corporate Transformation*, New York: Wiley.

Zuber-Skerritt, O. (1996), *New Directions in Action Research*, Brighton: Falmer Press.

10

Balancing Research and Action: Reflections on an Action Research Project in a Social Services Department

Jan Waterson

Keywords

Research; Action; Social services

Introduction

Action research seeks to combine social research with social action. This is not without its problems. (Everitt *et al.* 1992: 118)

Academics are frequently employed as contract researchers by service delivery organizations such as local government social services departments, with the expressed aim of some service developments emanating from the process. This type of research is frequently referred to in tender documents as action research, which is often viewed by non-researchers as being particularly relevant and apposite for practical contexts (Zuber-Skeritt 1996; Greenwood and Levin 1998; Stringer 1999). Consequently, the term "action research" may sometimes be used so broadly as to encompass any research designed to stimulate social change and learning (Hart and Bond 1995). The term was originally coined by Lewin in the USA, during the 1940s, and developed by other American social psychologists. Lewin built on the work of the Chicago philosopher John Dewey, who believed that the only real sources of knowledge were to be found in action. Essentially, it denoted a research approach that involved participants in a social experiment with the aim of achieving certain improvements (Lewin 1946). Work at the Tavistock Institute of Human Relations in the UK after the Second World War extended and promoted the model and there have been renewed interest and developments in this approach in the late 1990s (Hart and Bond 1995; Greenwood and Levin 1998; Stringer 1999).

Gomm *et al.* (2000) and Grbich (1999) distinguish action research by type of outcome sought, distinguishing community action research, action research for learning development, and action research change-management or organizational-development. The latter is the topic for this paper. This aims to make improvements in the way an organization functions, by working with the organizational actors in a cycle of action, data gathering, analysis, reflection and planning further action, as the researcher(s) and the organization work together (Menzies Lyth 1988; Vince 1996; Bowling 1997). Praxis and research go together, each taking account of the other, and influencing the way people think about an issue (Everitt *et al.* 1992). The process of the research and the relationships between all stakeholders become as important as substantive findings or solutions to the "problem" (Bryman 1989). Thus the researcher's role combines "importing" knowledge and enabling individuals to express the way they view the organization or change.

Although there are a few "behind the scenes" accounts of doing research (Bell and Roberts 1984; Shakespeare *et al.* 1993; Hobbs and May 1993), most accounts focus on the findings and present these as the result of a smooth planned process. Most published accounts of action research are "success" stories (Gomm *et al.* 2000), whereas this paper presents an alternative experience, using a case study of an action research project carried out for a local authority social services department under contract, as it sought to implement and deliver community care by developing care management between 1994 and 1997. The research aimed to describe and analyse key stakeholders' perceptions of the progress that had been made in terms of certain criteria, at three stages of development. The action in this context was to develop care management services in line with the findings of the research. At each stage extensive consultation was planned to follow the report to plan the next stage of development. The first cycle went as planned. The second did not, but the final stage recouped some lost ground. Nevertheless, although contractual relationships were fulfilled and research reports provided, the project gradually lost influence over departmental developments. This paper examines some issues that influenced that imbalance and the strategies used to counter them.

Background

During the mid-1990s local authorities were struggling to implement the NHS and Community Care Act 1990. This was to facilitate the partial privatization of local authority social care services, stimulating independent (private and not-for-profit) provision. Social services departments were to take a lead in assessing needs for social care and to purchase appropriate services, developing the social care market to encourage a much more varied range of direct service provision suitable for local needs. This required their commissioning and assessing, and providing functions to be separated. This usually meant that assessing and providing tasks which might have previously been delivered on an integrated basis for distinct client groups, were reorganized into distinct purchaser and provider sections (Lewis and Glennerster 1996). In order to deliver these new roles in the recently established social care market, staff were expected to develop new skills in management, customer care, business planning, contracting, commissioning and marketing.

There was no common understanding of what care management (the process whereby individual community care needs were to be managed) was, and a great diversity of implementation between authorities emerged (Lewis and Glennerster 1996). The government guidance spoke of care management as a process involving planning services, publishing information about services, assessing individuals needs, designing and ensuring care plans were implemented, monitored and reviewed (Department of Health 1991). Assessment was to be needs-led rather than service-led, but in the absence of a general model or local precedent, learning-by-doing was the only option.

In the department in question, care management had been introduced through a rolling programme involving a few teams at a time and supported by a task force set up expressly for that purpose and a few other related tasks, in line with some previous research, two years earlier. This approach was justified on the following grounds: policy could be developed through learning from experience; support resources could be concentrated on a few teams at a time; it was an opportunity for continuous evaluation; it allowed the introduction of gradual change through evolution. This situation, where the inputs were unspecific and outcomes uncertain, apparently fitted nicely with action research (Illsley 1980).

While senior management set the overall strategy, middle management and social workers implemented it. Social workers can be seen as "street-level bureaucrats", as concerned with the impact of policies upon their relationships with service users, as with acting as functionaries of the department (Lipsky 1980). Implementing policies is a key area where they exercise discretion (Butcher 1995; Hill 1997). In other words, they make policy (Hill 2000) and in the community care arena have been acknowledged as the most important but least acknowledged corporate communicators (Audit Commission 1995). Clearly the research had to encompass their activities as well as management's. Such a situation promised fertile research territory, for as Pawson and Tilley (1997) emphasize, one of the tasks of the researcher is to uncover the structure of the social relationships between service providers, in order to understand why we have the policies and practices that we do.

The department had already collected a range of routine monitoring data, for example, the number of assessments carried out, priority ratings, and numbers of cases pending, providing a quantitative overview. What appeared important in this context was to assess how the workers perceived the advantages and disadvantages of care management and any implementation issues; data not easily gathered through numeric means (Pollitt et al. 1990; Pope and Mays 1995). Contextual information to assist the change process, by enabling participants to gain a better understanding of their organization and their role within it (Easterby-Smith et al. 1991; Shaw 1999) was also needed.

Methods

The research reports were expected to document departmental progress, identify issues to be resolved and principal strategic questions facing the department, rather than specific points of operational detail. In other words, the research was to inform and contribute to the action, that is, the development of care management, at each of the three stipulated stages. While I had specifically wanted to work with service users, the department thought this inappropriate. Earlier research had concentrated on their perspectives and a number of other initiatives were taking place simultaneously. As the newly established relationship between assessing staff and those providing services was fundamental to the quality of care management I decided to work with the two groups in separate research cycles, first the assessors, then the providers. The third report was to look at both together. This methodological approach explicitly recognized the different perspectives of these crucial stakeholder groups. Senior management agreed to provide written feedback after each report as a basis for further consultation across the department before the next research cycle commenced.

The department was seeking to promote user empowerment, choice, needs-led assessments, tailor-made packages of care, value for money and the mixed economy of care, but had not operationalized these six concepts, or determined appropriate targets for progress by specified times. These were redefined, so that the research question at each stage became: how far had the development of care management enabled the realization of these goals?

At each stage available documentary data—policy statements, reports and operational guidelines—were examined first. It was important to be as inclusive as possible. Over 50 staff were involved in the first phase. About a third of the total number of assessor teams were selected, excluding those who had been involved in the earlier research. This was to ensure a geographical spread and to cover all user groups. Each team was interviewed as a group for approximately three hours each in total. A topic guide was used, but the format was open and unstructured to allow for maximum interchange. The remaining 18 teams were asked for written comments, but despite a telephone reminder, only three took up the offer. Key middle and senior managers were also interviewed.

The second phase concentrated on the issues facing in-house service providers. The procedure was much the same: individual interviews with managers of different seniority, responsible for providing services for specific client groups, and group interviews with staff groups from different types of services for different user groups. In all 45 people were involved.

The third phase did not involve an extended data-gathering exercise. Three key questions about the progress of care management in the department were used to frame a consultative exercise. These were taken from the conclusion of the previous report and there were two further questions about how user involvement could be promoted and what positive lessons could be learned from the way care management had been introduced to the department, and could be applied to future changes. A questionnaire on these five issues was produced, structured to give a numerical rating on progress to date. All managers with a responsibility for care management (assessing or providing) were asked to use it to consult as widely as possible with staff and service users and to represent those views at one of two consultation meetings, to which they were all invited.

In total, 51 managers, mainly from the assessor side, attended. Participants worked in small mixed groups, to identify what factors had helped development so far, in relation to each of the five issues and to suggest further constructive steps for the department to take to continue this progress. All participants were asked to leave completed copies of the questionnaire at the end of the workshop. Those who did not were subsequently reminded by telephone. Thirty-six completed questionnaires were finally returned and formed the basis of the third report.

Inheriting a Project

The first research dilemma was that this project was effectively inherited. There had been an earlier research project on the implementation of care management during the previous two years, in the course of which three reports had been provided by the person who held my academic post before me. Essentially I inherited a project-extension of another three years.

In fact, so had my colleagues in the social services department in question. The senior manager with overall responsibility for community care, who had set up the task force and the earlier research project, had left early in the previous year. The manager with specific responsibility for care management had left the previous summer and not been replaced. The task force manager and one project worker had also left the authority just after the extended research contract was agreed. Another worker had just been appointed manager and a further worker joined the project as I was doing my initial fieldwork.

The actual tender document was only one side of paper, giving very vague expectations of what was required. It stipulated that three action research reports assessing departmental progress in implementing care management were expected at yearly intervals. Each report was to be accompanied by a very short summary suitable for wide distribution with the authority, which I presumed was to be by way of feedback to all staff. The previous reports had been more consultative than research-based, which created an immediate difficulty for me.

The newly appointed manager of the task force, who was responsible for implementing the second research contract (her predecessor having negotiated it with the university before my arrival), resolved, with me, that, while some continuity with the previous work was needed, my own approach should be more systematic and analytical. To that end I summarized the issues raised in the earlier reports and we determined a series of topics to cover, in addition to others staff might raise. In fact, because we had all inherited the situation, this was resolved more easily than might have been the case if I had been a sole inheritor.

Multiple Agendas

On reflection there were multiple research agendas operating in this situation. My close relationship with the task force, who facilitated my access to departmental staff and documentation seemed a suitably sensible strategy at the time. After all, I needed a "product champion", but I also needed to be seen as an impartial, independent and critical observer and reflector (Everitt *et al.* 1992), able to seek out the issues of concern as seen by various stakeholders, and to represent them to others in the organization (Bowling 1997). I was aware that this was a complex task raising recognizable ethical dilemmas (British Sociological Association 1992). The task was to tailor the process to the research question, and to create knowledge in a reliable and trustworthy way (Hood *et al.* 1999). In this situation I knew my integrity as a researcher was paramount if I was to create mutual and reciprocal dialogue involving the exchange of both positive and negative views. Research seen as top-down, like any externally imposed change was likely to encounter resistance and indifference from middle managers and social workers (Casey 1993).

My strategy was to emphasize that the change to care management had been imposed by central government and that staff at all levels of the department needed to work together in the best interests of the service users. In the event I underestimated the strength of deeply held and conflicting roles and political sensitivities (Lee 1993). Ground-level staff were primarily preoccupied with their individual users' immediate needs:

> *"We'll try anything in the best interests of our clients."* (Social worker-assessor)

Care management, or indeed any innovation, was only useful in so far as it changed the "real issue", that is, improved user services. This was well recognized by middle management:

> *"If social workers cannot see tangible benefits in terms of improving quality of service for their clients they will resist change."* (Assessor team manager)

Social workers were seeing, quite realistically, that care management meant major threats to parts of their role that they had valued (National Institute of Social Work 1995; Hadley and Clough 1997). Assessors complained of being unable to influence service delivery in line with user needs, which to them was the advantage of care management, when elected members, because of ideological reasons, severely curtailed what could be obtained from the independent sector. They were similarly disillusioned about departmental systems of assessing unmet need which when collated were supposed to be used to stimulate services. Their verdict was that care management had not produced any substantial improvement, apart from domiciliary services, in the range or flexibility of service provision available.

Senior management had very different immediate priorities. They were juggling Department of Health requirements with those of the local authority as a whole and the demands of local politicians who were ideologically opposed to the philosophy of community care as introduced by the Conservative government.

The result was different views of the underlying aim of the research, and what was the research question. For the social workers it was mainly about improving user services, so the research question became: how can care management improve services? For senior management it was, first, how can our system meet government criteria? and, second, how can it reconcile that with the requirements of locally elected members? Of course the standard and range of services were important but they viewed them through the external lenses of central and local government pressures. The strategy adopted was to recognize and point out these differences at feedback and consultation meetings and in the reports. This appeared to work until after the second report when issues became too sensitive and the difference too wide for the conflict to be managed. It is well known that action research requires an understanding of group processes and change management, but most of the change management literature assumes that the change agents are the powerful organizational players and that the direction of change is in line with management policy (Broome 1998). This was not the case here, when I failed to represent the validity of the perceptions of provider social workers to senior management who had other agendas to deal with.

Changes in Organizational Personnel and Roles

Any organization is liable to be constantly changing. Action research can be like trying to document a moving target. In this instance, organizational change had been continuous and far-reaching, providing a constantly uncertain context. Immediately before I started my research there had been major changes in the senior management, and in the staffing of the implementation task force. A new director took up post while I was doing the assessor fieldwork, the post having been filled by an acting director for the previous year. The department then reorganized, with immediate job implications for all senior management.

Significant staff changes created a lack of leadership for community care in general and for the implementation of care management and the work of the task force in particular. The acting assistant director with overall responsibility for community care left, but was permanently appointed to the position three months later. Despite the interim cover provided by other members of the senior management team, care management and the work of the development task force did not rank highly in departmental concerns.

The task force itself was abolished immediately after reorganization. As might be expected in the period before this reorganization, the project workers, like many others, were concerned about their future employment status. From the research's point of view its "product champions" were less active, and access to departmental staff during this phase was more difficult than previously, but contacts made during the first research cycle proved helpful. I requested that a steering group be set up for the third cycle, but the director decided it should be directly managed by the two assistant directors responsible for assessors and providers. Neither had time to facilitate access to staff and it was decided that lengthy fieldwork was inappropriate and resources would be better used in a participative consultative exercise for all assessing and providing staff.

This changeable situation also had advantages. Departmental staff did not see me as a management stooge. Many of them were unsure who was actually managing the introduction of care management or the task force. As the manager of a day-care service complained:

> *"I'm acting up, my assistant team manager is acting up, my manager is acting up and his manager is acting up. Who's in charge? My team couldn't name managers above my manager. They disengage and become demoralized. The conspiracy theory runs wild, probably with no reason. The message to us is you can't plan ahead. You'll possibly get a new manager soon, but we can't tell you who that'll be."*

As in other authorities, workers were tired, stressed and negative about the rapidity of change (National Institute of Social Work 1995). As one team member put it:

> *"It could all change tomorrow so why invest in it?"*

They were referring to departmental changes, but I was acutely aware they could have been referring to participation in the research. Demoralization was more widespread amongst provider staff, who were understandably anxious about their job prospects, wondering how they could compete in an open social care market, when their overheads were considerably higher than their independent rivals. As one manager observed:

> *"People don't think about development work if they're anxious whether their job's going to be there in two months time."* (Provider team manager)

Not surprisingly it was difficult to be certain that they were not confusing simultaneous changes and uncertainties with the introduction of care management. It was necessary when working with staff to keep reminding them of the focus of the work. It was also inevitable that their predominantly negative feelings about other changes would colour perceptions of care management. The strategy for dealing with this was to draw attention to these dynamics explicitly in face-to-face work and in the reports.

Issues in Presenting Findings

The literature indicates that managers often want research outcomes translated into a few immediate policy recommendations which will solve the "problem", whereas grassroots workers are inclined to dismiss such recommendations with cynicism (Pollitt *et al.* 1990). In reality, research may clarify issues but usually indicates several alternative potential recommendations. In view of the need to achieve some discussion and consensus about the research findings no specific recommendations other than about the process for feedback and dissemination were made. It was requested that all individuals and teams who had participated should receive a complete report and that separate consultation meetings for staff concerned with each client group should be held. Both were to facilitate feedback on validity and to identify pertinent issues for the following phase of action research.

Presenting what was viewed as positive was easy. Achievement was affirming. Moreover, problems identified as blocking the process of innovation, which could be relatively simply resolved, for example by specific policy guidance, training, or changed administrative procedures were identified. Complaints, disenchantment and negativity, which were not infrequent, created a problem of how to present them, if at all, in the report. As Gomm *et al.* (2000) note, much action research is participative or collaborative and the natural tendency is to minimize conflicts. However, there was a remarkable unanimity of view amongst social workers and middle managers in the first two stages, which suggested a certain validity of findings. The issue was how to avoid collusion and present differences positively. For example, one middle manager observed:

> *"The task force was not linked into operational management but to the departmental senior manager and the team managers. When the senior manager went all the "umph" went out of it. There was a lack of leadership and vision. It was a vacuum and we'd been taking a cautious line before that. Three senior management posts went down to one. It was a hiatus at a time of cultural change just when you need to take people with you."*

The research needed to be true to its data and participants, but I was wary of senior management response. This reaction was presented, but defined as a need for continuity of leadership and vision rather than as a very thinly veiled complaint about senior management. The nature of this type of research, designed to reflect different subjectivities, and analyse how different departmental actors saw the major issues in providing quality care management, was stressed. Inevitably some would be at variance with each other.

It was more difficult in the second "provider" report to reframe a situation where there was a cultural legacy of underinvestment of both human and financial resources. As in many authorities, there was a distinct reality in comments that provider staff had a lower status than their assessor colleagues (Lewis and Glennerster 1996). Similarly it would have been dishonest to ignore the evidence that, while many providers aspire to provide individualized care packages, resource levels made this impossible. The chosen strategy emphasized that this was not unique to this authority but a national situation, created externally.

Many grassroots staff were dubious about the rolling programme of implementation, with its "bottoms up" tactic, which, although producing creative responses, was seen as "doing management's job for them". The task group's work had emphasized the dissemination of good practice but for most staff, at all levels, there was no obvious cycle of encouraging innovatory practice, evaluating it, analysing its transferability to other situations, and defining and codifying what was appropriate at client group or departmental level. There did not appear to be any obvious transfer process to mainstream operations. This uncertain picture was presented in the second report, but to move forward from this negative scene key questions facing the department were identified. These were designed to emphasize the wider policy context and were purposefully phrased in neutral language:

1. How could a previously underdeveloped sector be "jump-started" so that a uniformly high level of services would be provided, and establishments would be able to compete in a more open market at a time of financial cutbacks?
2. How could services become more tailored to individual needs in a climate of increasing economic stringency?
3. How could assessors and providers continue to develop their roles simultaneously and in partnership?

It was also suggested that a review of the management of change in the department might be helpful as many of the "problems" identified seemed to be related to organizational style rather than the introduction of care management itself.

Dissemination and Feedback Issues

After the first report a wide-ranging consultation process took place. Almost 200 staff involved in assessment, middle management, senior management, members of the task force and representatives from the user involvement forums, specialist carers' unit and the voluntary sector were involved in five separate meetings, each concentrating on one particular user group. These were intended to promote communication, dialogue and feedback, and to plan future work. These were hardworking and enthusiastic occasions, facilitated by senior management. The report was welcomed, endorsed, and the findings validated with no challenges, but echoed and emphasized. For me the greatest satisfaction was hearing one middle manager say:

> "The social workers will recognize and own this [the report]."

By the time the second phase was under way, many of the general issues raised had been addressed in revised departmental documentation. Research and action had been nicely balanced and integrated.

After submitting my draft for the second report I was reminded that research is a negotiated and political activity framed by power relationships and on constantly shifting ground (Hood et al. 1999). Grinyer (1995) emphasizes that great pressure can be brought to bear on researchers in situations where research exposes and challenges those in powerful positions, but I was unprepared. I was summoned to a meeting with the senior management team to discuss my draft report, which had been presented in a similar way to the first. The new director, who I had not met, criticized my approach and complained that there were no numeric data in the report. He appeared more familiar with a genre of consultative exercises, written from a positivistic deductive perspective, supported by statistical data, and with clear recommendations specifying "the answer", than with qualitative action research. The literature shows that many managers are resistant to dispassionate analysis and reflection; concentrating on short-term management of the political agendas is more important (Pollitt et al. 1990; Clarke et al. 1994; Clark and Newman 1997). For those whose working lives are dominated by quick-turn-round time scales, tight terms of reference, numbers and specific outcomes, working in a culture where "real" managers impose their will (Flynn 1997), an interpretist approach could appear alien. My justifications and discussion of reliability, validity, and rigorous empirical grounding failed to bridge this gap. The closure of the task force had created an absence of an internal "product champion" at this stage, which was also unhelpful.

In retrospect, it is much easier to appreciate the scale of the demands and unfamiliar expectations that were being imposed on senior managers and to understand that "disarray verging on chaos" was very common in social services departments in the mid-1990s (Hadley and Clough 1997). In a context of declining resources, how to manage the externally imposed change was a major dilemma for them (Lewis and Glennerster 1996). To give credence to critical and negative reports from staff was likely to be yet an extra problem.

I discussed my draft with the ex-manager of the task force, now working in a neighbouring department, who thought the findings "were to be expected". I was also convinced that it was a fair representation. I considered resigning from the project, feeling that my integrity as a researcher was being undermined, but was mindful that it was bringing in much-needed income to my department and would help in the RAE assessment.

In the end there was a gap of several months before my final report was submitted and a new paragraph inserted in the introduction at the senior management's insistence:

> The dissemination of this report, although the findings relate to the period immediately before reorganization, has been delayed until the initial shock waves of reorganization have had time to settle and other concerns such as the management of care re-emerge . . . Some months into reorganization it seems that the provider side has taken a massive leap forward and is beginning to grasp the nettle of change.

Eventually, the report and its accompanying short summary was only circulated to a small number of senior managers, not to the staff I had worked with, as I had requested.

Feedback on the final consultation process itself was positive. The review questionnaire was thought to be clear and easy to follow, but I was again surprised by the social services department's response to my draft report, which this time contained numeric data, albeit representing subjective staff perception ratings of development. After I had furnished it, I was unexpectedly absent from the university for a number of months. When I returned I was surprised to find no response. Eventually written comments on it were produced by the department and incorporated into the final report which was finally submitted almost a year after the consultation workshops. I do not know whether it was circulated or what action resulted. My suspicion is that the changes in "product champion" to lead the innovation would have made development unlikely (Stocking 1985).

Jan Waterson

Was the Research Useful?

While organizations do not stay still waiting for research reports to be finished, questions about the usefulness of research carried out by an outsider in such situations need to be raised. Certainly action research is a dynamic approach and can be suited to dynamic situations, provided it remains centre stage and does not drift to the wings of the enterprise, as happened here.

All ground staff and middle management were clear that any research must be independent and neutral, thus avoiding any suspicions of vested interest if carried out in-house. For them, the role of the "friendly outsider" (Greenwood and Levin 1998) was welcome. The reports and ensuing consultations confirmed and clarified things that they had experienced individually. The process sharpened their thinking and analytical skills, encouraged them to be more confident in valuing their opinions and experiences, and to co-generate meaning and ideas for the future. They obviously valued their involvement as shown by the comments in box 1.

I do not know whether the research was useful for senior staff. Certainly, the home-grown intelligence and knowledge across the agency, which was able to recognize achievements and also identify gaps and issues in policy development, was a considerable resource and was precisely the sort of response I had aimed for. Several social workers said they would have valued a researcher working full-time with the task force, which I took as an endorsement of the value of action research.

Shortcomings were related to the use made of the information. As one assessor commented:

"It's great to have a voice, but it depends on what action is taken afterwards."

The final consultations suggested that in future action research, the organization should plan development, research and any implementation together. Securing more resources for social care, opposing the development of a market in social care or persuading local politicians to work with central

---

Box 1

"It's an opportunity to get a general feel of what is going on across the agency, which is sometimes difficult." (Provider)

"One of the few opportunities for formal feedback to senior management about changes that have/are being made." (Assessor manager)

"It was very useful to meet in combined assessor and provider groups about common issues and to review how far we had come." (Assessor)

"I will follow up on areas where I have given a low score to Departmental progress." (Provider manager)

---

government were beyond the scope of the research, but this experience demonstrated that action research could be part of

"a plan to win hearts and minds, encouraging staff to own developments." (Assessor team manager)

For me, as the researcher, I reflected on my own action (Schon 1983), developing my ideas for this paper, and I learned a great deal about defensible decisions on systematic and ethical processes (see Kemshall, this volume) in large-scale action research. Linking my importation of knowledge of the wider issues, in policy implementation and care management particularly, to local knowledge enhanced my theoretical understanding. I wrote three substantial reports, which could be used for publications, and I developed useful data sets for teaching purposes.

Conclusion

The researcher's primary task in this sort of operation is: to illuminate "taken-for-granted" meanings; to act as "honest communicator" in opening up communication between different insider viewpoints; to clarify; to analyse; to act as "honest broker" representing differences; to suggest ways of negotiating between them; and to make findings known. As with producing a meal, there is no "right" outcome to action research, but many alternatives.

In this instance, issues of inheriting a project, multiple agendas, changes in key organizational staff, problems of how to present findings, and dilemmas about dissemination and feedback created predicaments for the researcher and distorted the balance between action and research. In addition, as Vince (1996) observes, action research is about change and is just as likely to produce defensive resistance or encourage retrospective nostalgia (Gabriel 1993). As this paper demonstrates, organizational morale cannot be ignored (Reason 1994).

Finally, what would I recommend to other researchers embarking on similar projects? I would use an independent mentor, bring in a co-worker, be more proactively in contact with senior management, and establish a steering group with an external researcher involved. I would emphasize very much more explicitly from the outset the sort of research model involved, I would stress that commissioners may not like independent findings, discuss strategies for recognizing the validity of all co-participants', including "street-level bureaucrats", contributions, ways of handling conflict, and emphasize that research findings alone will not promote change.

References

Audit Commission (1995), *The Community Revolution: Personal Social Services and Community Care*, London: Audit Commission.

Bell, C., and Roberts, H. (eds) (1984), *Social Researching: Politics, Problems and Practice*, London: Routledge and Kegan Paul.

Bowling, A. (1997), *Research Methods in Health: Investigating Health and Health Services*, Buckingham: Open University Press.

Jan Waterson

British Sociological Association (1992), Statement of ethical practice, *Sociology*, 26, 4: 703–7.
Broome, A. (1998), *Managing Change*, 2nd edn, Basingstoke: Macmillan.
Bryman, A. (1989), *Research Methods and Organization Studies*, London: Allen and Unwin.
Bulmer, M. (1982), *The Uses of Social Research*, London: Allen and Unwin.
Butcher, T. (1995), *Delivering Welfare: The Governance of Social Services in the 1990s*, Buckingham: Open University Press.
Casey, D. (1993), *Managing Learning in Organizations*, Buckingham: Open University Press.
Clarke, J., Cochrane, A., and McLaughlin, E. (1994), *Managing Social Policy*, Buckingham: Open University Press.
Clarke, J., and Newman, J. (1997), *The Managerial State*, London: Sage.
Department of Health (1991), *Care Management and Assessment: Practitioners' Guide*, London: HMSO.
Easterby-Smith, M., Thorpe, R., and Lowe, A. (1991), *Management Research: An Introduction*, London: Sage.
Everitt, A., Hardiker, P., Littlewood, J., and Mullender, A. (1992), *Applied Research for Better Practice*, London: Macmillan.
Flynn, N. (1997), *Public Sector Management*, 2nd edn, Hemel Hempstead: Prentice Hall and Harvester Wheatsheaf.
Gabriel, Y. (1993), Organization nostalgia: reflections on the "golden age". In S. Fineman (ed.), *Emotion in Organizations*, London: Sage.
Gomm, R., Needham, G., and Bulman, A. (2000), *Evaluating Research in Health and Social Care*, London: Sage.
Grbich, C. (1999), *Qualitative Research in Health*, London: Sage.
Greenwood, D. J., and Levin, M. (1998), *Introduction to Action Research: Social Research for Social Change*, London: Sage.
Grinyer, A. (1995), Risk, the real world and naïve sociology. In J. Gabe (ed.), *Medicine, Health and Risk: Sociological Approaches*, Oxford: Blackwell.
Hadley, R., and Clough, R. (1997), *Care in Chaos: Frustration and Challenge in Community Care*, London: Cassell.
Hart, E., and Bond, M. (1995), *Action Research in Health and Social Care: a Guide to Practice*, Buckingham: Open University Press.
Hill, M. (1997), *Understanding Social Policy*, 5th edn, Blackwell: Oxford.
Hill, M. (2000), *Understanding Social Policy*, 6th edn, Blackwell: Oxford.
Hobbs, D., and May, T. (eds) (1993), *Interpreting the Field: Accounts of Ethnography*, Oxford: Oxford University Press.
Hood, S., Mayall, B., and Oliver, S. (1999), *Critical Issues in Social Research: Power and Prejudice*, Buckingham: Open University Press.
Illsley, R. (1980), *Professional or Public Health? Sociology in Health and Medicine*, London: Nuffield Provincial Hospitals Trust.
Lee, R. (1993), *Doing Research on Sensitive Topics*, London: Sage.
Lewin, K. (1946), Action research and minority problems, *Journal of Social Issues*, 2: 34–46.
Lewis, J., and Glennerster, H. (1996), *Implementing Community Care*, Buckingham: Open University Press.
Lipsky, M. (1980), *Street-level Bureaucracy*, New York: Russell Sage.
Menzies Lyth, I. (1988), *Containing Anxiety in Institutions: Selected Essays, Vol. 1*, London: Free Association Books.
National Institute for Social Work (1995), *Working in the Social Services*, London: NISW.
Pawson, R., and Tilley, N. (1997), *Realistic Evaluation*, 2nd edn, London: Sage.
Pollitt, C., Harrison, S., Hunter, D. J., and Marnoch, G. (1990), No Hiding Place: On the Discomforts of Researching the Contemporary Policy Process, *Journal of Social Policy*, 19, 2: 169–90.

Pope, C., and Mays, N. (1995), Researching the parts other methods cannot reach: an introduction to qualitative methods in health and health service research, *British Medical Journal*, 311: 42–5.

Reason, P. (1994), *Participation in Human Inquiry*, London: Sage.

Schon, D. A. (1983), *The Reflective Practitioner*, New York: Basic Books.

Shakespeare, P., Atkinson, D., and French, S. (eds) (1993), *Reflecting on Research Practice*, Buckingham: Open University Press.

Shaw, I. (1999), *Qualitative Evaluation*, London: Sage.

Stocking, B. (1985), *Initiative and Inertia: Case Studies in the NHS*, London: Nuffield Provincial Hospital Trust.

Stringer, E. T. (1999), *Action Research: A Handbook for Practitioners*, 2nd edn, London: Sage.

Vince, R. (1996), *Managing Change: Reflections on Equality and Management Learning*, Bristol: Policy Press.

Zuber-Skerritt, O. (1996), *New Directions in Action Research*, London: Falmer Press.

NOTES ON CONTRIBUTORS

Paul Bate is Professor of Health Services Management Development at the Health Services Management Centre, University of Birmingham.

Dawn Chatty is Deputy Director and Dulverton Senior Research Fellow at the Refugee Studies Centre, Queen Elizabeth House, University of Oxford.

Elizabeth Ettorre is Professor of Sociology at the University of Plymouth.

Catherine Jones Finer is Reader in Comparative Social Policy at the University of Birmingham and Editor of *Social Policy & Administration*.

Hazel Kemshall is Professor of Community and Criminal Justice in the Department of Social and Community Studies, De Montfort University.

Gillian Lewando Hundt is Professor of Social Sciences in Health at the University of Warwick.

Janet Lewis is Director of Research at the Joseph Rowntree Foundation.

Jessica Ogden is Lecturer in the Department of Public Health and Policy at the London School of Hygiene and Tropical Medicine.

John Porter is Senior Lecturer in the Department of Infectious and Tropical Diseases at the London School of Hygiene and Tropical Medicine.

Hilary Third is Research Fellow in the School of Planning and Housing in the Edinburgh College of Art, Heriot-Watt University.

Jan Waterson is Lecturer in the Department of Social Policy and Social Work, University of Birmingham.

INDEX

Index

Index

partnership 12, *125*; definitions of 13–14; development of 17, 22–4; in health sector 14; North/South relationship 14, 24; practitioner/academic expertise 70; use of term 15
Pearson, L. B. 13
politics 100–3
PPP 2
Project 96 29–41
Proust, M. 114

Realizing our potential (1993), White Paper 3
research, activity of 1; assessment of 4, 8–10; funding of 1–3, 6–8; management of 5–6; and normative assumptions 102–3; open-ended invitations 69–73; qualitative 57–8; relevance of 3–4, 10, 11; users/beneficiaries 3–5; as value-driven 105–6
Research Assessment Exercise (RAE) 2, 6, 7, 40, 94, 139; role/effect of 8–10
research management 27; clear leadership 29–30; equality of partners 30; preparation 28–9; structure/basic tasks 30–1, *32*; successful 28
researcher/researched relationship 76; culture/language differences 72–3, 79–80; divergent expectations 70, 73; hagiography/propaganda aspects 71–2; informal understanding 69–70
Revised National Tuberculosis Control Programme (RNTCP) 18, 19, 24
risk, of challenge 103; and commitment to ethical codes of conduct/principles 107; normative assumptions 102–3; in penal policy 101
risk society 101
Rothschild Report (1971) 40
Rough Sleepers Initiative (RSI) 83, 84, 87, 89, 90

Rough Sleepers Unit 84
rough sleeping 95; quantifying 87–9; research in 83–4

Schein, E. 115
Scotland, homelessness in *see* homelessness
Scottish Higher Education Funding Council 3
Scottish Social Inclusion Network 97
Shelter (Scotland) 83, 87
Social Science Research council (SSRC) 2
social services research, background 130–1; changes in organizational personnel/roles 135–6; dissemination/feedback issues 138–9; inheriting a project 133; issues in presenting findings 136–8; methods 131–3; multiple agendas 133–5; as useful 140–1
Swedish International Development Agency (SIDA) 17

Tavistock Institute of Human Relations 115, 129
Teaching Quality Assessment (TQA) 8
tuberculosis (TB), background 16–17; DFID programme 17; revised National Programme in India 17–18; terms of reference for operations research 18–19

United Nations Relief and Works Agency (UNRWA) 56
United Nations (UN) 85

Vince, R. 141

Webb, S. 87
Wellcome Trust 2
West, Morris 78, 79
World Health Organization (WHO) 17